TREASURES OF
ANCIENT EGYPT

TREASURES OF
ANCIENT EGYPT

Nigel Fletcher-Jones

This edition first published in 2024

First published in 2019

Published by Amber Books Ltd
United House
North Road
London N7 9DP
United Kingdom
www.amberbooks.co.uk
Instagram: amberbooksltd
Facebook: www.facebook.com/amberbooks
Twitter: @amberbooks

Copyright © 2019 Amber Books Ltd.

All rights reserved. With the exception of quoting brief passages for the purpose of review no part of this publication may be reproduced without prior written permission from the publisher. The information in this book is true and complete to the best of our knowledge. All recommendations are made without any guarantee on the part of the author or publisher, who also disclaim any liability incurred in connection with the use of this data or specific details.

ISBN: 978-1-83886-464-4

Project Editor: Michael Spilling
Design: Hart McLeod Ltd
Picture Research: Terry Forshaw and Susannah Jayes

Printed in China

CONTENTS

INTRODUCTION	6
THE OLD KINGDOM	12
THE MIDDLE KINGDOM	52
THE NEW KINGDOM	80
THE LATE PERIOD	158
THE GRECO-ROMAN PERIOD	178
TIMELINE AND MAP	222
ACKNOWLEDGEMENTS/PICTURE CREDITS	224

Introduction

Few cultures have left behind as many immediately recognizable objects and buildings as ancient Egypt. The gold mask of Tutankhamun, the plastered limestone bust of Nefertiti, the pyramids and the Great Sphinx at Giza, the rock-cut temples at Abu Simbel, the Rosetta Stone, the Valley of the Kings, and the vast temple complexes at Karnak and Luxor can all be quickly conjured up in the mind's eye.

Even less specific objects, such as the *nemes* – the striped headcloth worn by pharaohs – or the close-fitting vulture headdress worn by queens, the mummy in its wrappings, lion-headed goddesses, falcon-headed gods and the cross-like *ankh* hieroglyph symbolizing life, all are immediately familiar.

Indeed, many of the towns and cities in North America and Europe contain buildings – especially those built between the mid-nineteenth century and the first half of the twentieth century – that mimic the columns and other architectural features of ancient Egyptian temples, as a direct result of the explosion of interest in ancient Egypt between the publication of the *Description de l'Egypte* in France between 1809 and 1822 and the years following the discovery of Tutankhamun's tomb by Howard Carter in 1922.

FAMILIAR OBJECTS

Treasures of Ancient Egypt is a celebration of many of these familiar objects, together with some less familiar ones, that complete a brief overview of the long and fascinating history of this most special of civilizations. Before we begin this story, a word must be said about

OPPOSITE:
The Funerary Mask of Tutankhamun
This iconic object, from the tomb of Tutankhamun (1336–1327 BC) in the Valley of the Kings, protected the upper part of the mummy. The young king's face is surrounded by the royal striped *nemes* headdress, which is made of gold and glass paste (imitating lapis lazuli). On his forehead, the two guardian deities of Upper and Lower Egypt – Nekhbet (the vulture) and Wadjet (the striking cobra) – signify the king's authority over the whole country. The curved false beard indicates the divine status of the deceased. (Grand Egyptian Museum, Cairo.)

names and dates. Many of the most familiar names associated with ancient Egypt – the goddess Isis, the god Osiris, the capital city of Memphis and the temple city of Thebes, for example – are not Egyptian names, but Greek. I have kept these names here rather than their Egyptian equivalents, simply because they are so familiar to us today.

For the names of kings, however, I have used the Egyptian name despite the fact that we cannot know exactly how they were spelled or pronounced because a sense of the vowel sounds is largely absent from hieroglyphic texts. In this manner, Amenophis III is referred to here as Amenhotep III, and Thutmosis III becomes Thutmose III – alongside other wholly Egyptian names such as Rameses, Tutankhamun, Akhenaten and the female king, Hatshepsut.

A QUESTION OF TIME

Prior to 690 BC, there are no exact dates of events in ancient Egyptian history. In their writings, the Egyptians measured the annual passing of time only by 'regnal years' – the number of years the current king had sat on the throne.

Around the year 300 BC, Manetho (an Egyptian priest writing in Greek) attempted to bring order to the long royal history of ancient Egypt by grouping kings into 30 dynasties based on the familial or political ties of pharaohs.

There have been arguments about this list ever since: we believe some listed kings probably did not exist; others, who we know from the archaeological record did exist, aren't present in the list. This does not provide a firm basis for establishing the reigns of individual pharaohs with any degree of precision. The well-known king Rameses II, for example, will be said in this book to have reigned between 1279 and 1213 BC, but the reader may also see the spans 1290–1223 BC and 1265–1200 BC stated in other books with equal conviction. In the great timespan occupied by the Egyptian state, such tiny discrepancies must surely be forgivable.

In addition to dynasties, Egyptologists make use of broader divisions of Egyptian history starting with the formation of the Egyptian state in the *Early Dynastic Period* (approximately 3100–2686 BC), followed by the *Old Kingdom* (2686–2181 BC); an unsettled period known as the *First Intermediate Period* (2181–1985 BC); the *Middle Kingdom* (1985–1650 BC); another unsettled period known as the *Second Intermediate Period* (1650–1550 BC); the *New Kingdom* (1550–1069 BC); the *Third Intermediate Period* (1069–747 BC); and the *Late Period* (747–332 BC), which saw the increasing involvement of the Persian Empire until it took control of Egypt directly in 342 BC. The Persians were defeated in 332 BC by Alexander the Great, who inaugurated the *Hellenistic Period* (332–30 BC), including the rule of the Greek Ptolemies, which lasted until the *Roman Period* of 30 BC to AD 395. For convenience, these last two are grouped together in this book as the *Greco-Roman Period*.

OPPOSITE:
The Great Temple, Abu Simbel
Entirely carved into riverside cliffs in the far south of Egypt, the Great and Small Temples at Abu Simbel entered the world's consciousness when they were threatened by the construction of the Aswan High Dam. Through a massive international effort, the two temples were dismantled and moved to higher ground between 1964 and 1968. They were constructed on the order of Rameses II (1279–1213 BC), and form a rare combination of twin temples for a pharaoh and his Great Wife (in this case, Nefertari).

OPPOSITE:

The Pyramid of Khaefre and the Great Sphinx, Giza Plateau

The second largest of the pyramids on the Giza plateau, the pyramid of Khaefre (2558–2532 BC) gives a clear idea of how an ancient Egyptian pyramid was built and what it looked like. The bulk of the structure was composed of locally quarried limestone, and then finished with fine, white, polished Tura limestone from quarries across the Nile (seen here at the top of the pyramid). The Great Sphinx was carved from a rock outcrop, and is generally accepted to be a representation of King Khaefre with a lion's body.

ABOVE:

Pectoral of the Goddess Nut, Tomb of Tutankhamun

This pectoral (or, perhaps, fitting for a belt) was found in the Anubis shrine in Tutankhamun's tomb. The wings of the sky goddess, Nut, are outstretched to surround the names of Tutankhamun (within the oval cartouches). The hieroglyphic text states that the goddess 'opens her arms over her son, the king, in protection of his body'. It is thought that this may have originally been made for Tutankhamun's father, Akhenaten. (Grand Egyptian Museum, Cairo.)

The Old Kingdom

During the period between 16,000 and 6000 years ago, the area now known as the Sahara was covered not by sand, but by grasslands and lakes – home to nomadic hunter-gatherer-fishers.

We can catch a tantalizing glimpse of the lives of some of these peoples from the caves at Wadi Sura ('Valley of the Pictures') about 600km (370 miles) west of the Nile. Here in the 'Cave of the Swimmers' and 'Cave of the Beasts' are images of figures hunting, running, dancing and what appears to be swimming. Accompanying these figures we can also see elephants, giraffes, ostriches and gazelles, alongside wild cattle – representing the herds that may have been 'managed' in some manner by these people.

Within this wider grassland landscape, the Nile Valley was regularly visited by the nomadic and semi-nomadic peoples who fished, gathered oysters, captured waterfowl and hunted along its banks, or gathered roots, tubers, and wild grains while living seasonally on sandbanks above the river waters.

NILE SETTLEMENTS

About 5500 BC, wheat, barley, sheep and goats were introduced to the Nile Valley from southwest Asia via the Sinai Peninsula, and at about the same time – due to a shift in climate patterns that drove the rain belts south – the grasslands away from the river disappeared as the desert emerged. Groups of people were increasingly pressed against the Nile, and their world became gradually divided between *deshret*, the 'Red Land' (the Western and Eastern Deserts) and *kemet*, the 'Black Land' (the Nile Valley).

It is not entirely clear whether the villages that sprang up along the Nile were permanent or seasonal settlements, but the growing population was increasingly dependent on wheat, barley and flax (from which linen

OPPOSITE:
Cave of the Swimmers, Wadi Sura
The area now covered by the Sahara was formerly savanna grassland. Now deep in Egypt's Western Desert, the Neolithic cave paintings at Wadi Sura show hunter-gatherer-fishers occupied in a variety of activities, including, possibly, swimming in the seasonal lakes.

was produced) that was harvested in the late winter or early spring, and on domesticated cattle, pigs, sheep and goats – although fishing and hunting for wildfowl, ostriches (whose eggs were used to create jewellery) and hippopotamus were also important.

Sea and land trade routes – aided by the domestication of the donkey – to and from Levant (the eastern Mediterranean coast) saw increasing imports of wood, incense, wine, and oil, and by around 3800 BC Egyptians were smelting the copper that was to become a major component of everyday life.

Related to this profitable trade, an elite emerged along the Nile that developed a desire for ever more costly jewellery and cosmetics. Carnelian, ivory, and garnet were fashioned into jewellery, and gold (derived at first from nuggets washed out from streams in the Eastern Desert) was soon combined with semi-precious lapis lazuli stones imported via Byblos (in modern Lebanon) from distant Afghanistan, to create those characteristic objects that imitated the bright sun and the deep blue sky of Egypt.

THE FIRST KINGS OF EGYPT

Well-ordered towns soon began to develop that were incorporated into confederations for purposes of trade and defence, and, over time, two centres began to dominate: Hierakonpolis in the south and Buto in the north. These centres adopted emblems of a white crown, the water lily (or 'lotus') and the vulture goddess Nekhbet in the south, and the red crown, the papyrus plant and the cobra goddess Wadjet in the north.

At some time around 3100 BC, the southern kingdom conquered the northern realms and united Egypt for the first time. There is debate whether this was under the king simply known as 'Scorpion', or King Narmer, or his son Aha. However, the spectacular slate cosmetic palette found at Hierakonpolis – showing Narmer wearing the White Crown of Upper (southern) Egypt on one side, and the Red Crown of Lower (northern) Egypt on the other – is generally accepted as indicating that the unification of Egypt took place either during or close to his reign.

As the power of the kings increased, so did the desire for wealth, and King Narmer sent out expeditions to exploit the resources of the new state. Along the Wadi Hammamat, these expeditions left their inscriptions as they gathered amethysts, malachite and slate from the region to the east of the river in the name of the king.

Also at around this time, the great trading post on Elephantine Island (in modern Aswan) opened for business for exotic products – including gold and ivory – from Nubia and further south within the African interior.

Under King Narmer (or King Aha), the capital of the newly united kingdom moved to Memphis (to the southwest of modern Cairo). This new city, created on land reclaimed from the Nile, lay on the boundary between Upper and Lower Egypt, and became the long-serving administrative capital of ancient Egypt.

The kings of this early period and for the next three centuries continued to be interred in the ancestral grounds at Abydos in the south. The new administrators of the capital – increasingly able to leave a record of their honours and achievements in the rapidly

OPPOSITE:
River Nile
The Nile flows from south to north. Consequently, the southern part of Egypt is known as 'Upper Egypt', and the northern part as 'Lower Egypt'. Ancient Egyptian civilization would not have arisen without the annual late-summer flooding of the Nile and the thick deposits of rich alluvial soil that were deposited on the river banks.

developing hieroglyphic script – were buried on the highlands west of Memphis in mud-brick, bench-like buildings, containing a small chapel and an underground burial chamber known as *mastabas*. These may have reflected, in part, the structures in which the kings themselves were buried at Abydos, where a visible mound covered in white plaster surmounted the burial chamber – perhaps reminiscent of the hill that, according to Egyptian myth, rose out of the primeval waters at the creation.

This earliest period most probably ended in civil war, but by the reign of King Djoser (2667–2648 BC), the country was reunited, and Djoser made the decision to be buried near his capital city of Memphis.

THE ORIGIN OF PYRAMIDS

As the wealth of the king's courtiers had increased, so the mastaba tombs in which they were buried became more elaborate – including, in some case, the addition of a second stepped layer. Unsurprisingly, the royal tombs also grew to enormous proportions – the mastaba burial complex of Djoser's father Khasekhemwy at Abydos, for example, measured 70m (230ft) along its longest wall and contained 43 storerooms. Not to be outdone, Djoser worked closely with the great architect Imhotep on the construction of his tomb at Saqqara, overlooking Memphis.

The initial concept of Djoser's new tomb was simple. It would be similar to his father's resting place at Abydos, but made of local limestone rather than mud-brick. The centrepiece, covering the burial chamber 28m (92ft) below, was to be a squat square structure. When built, this apparently made sufficient impression on both king and architect – or perhaps it wasn't quite visible enough from down in the valley – that three more layers, decreasing in size, were added, and then two more, to create a structure with six high steps. The resulting Step Pyramid, the precursor of all pyramids in Egypt and Nubia, stood 64m (210ft) high.

Next to this structure, a number of other buildings were added to the complex (rather than at a distance from the burial site as had been the tradition). Here Djoser and Imhotep mimicked, in stone, the wood and mud-brick palace that had served the living king in the valley below. The interior walls of the palace within the funerary complex were also covered in 36,000 exquisite turquoise tiles creating a reed pattern.

Buildings within the wider complex – some duplicated to the north and south to represent the king's dominion over all the country – were protected for eternity by the head of the cobra goddess Wadjet. Similarly positioned north to south was a ceremonial 140m (460ft) running track, upon which the king was expected to continue to prove his worthiness. In any case, he was to be well supplied in death – some 400 storerooms were constructed underground, containing vast quantities of barley, wheat, figs and grapes.

As would prove an enduring characteristic of Egyptian history, most of Djoser's immediate successors reigned for too short a time to build pyramids in imitation of his work.

The next great pyramid builder was the first king of the Fourth Dynasty, Seneferu (2613–2589 BC), who built not one, but three large structures. The first, an attempt to convert a

OPPOSITE:

Narmer Palette, Hierakonpolis
One of the greatest treasures in the Egyptian Museum, Cairo, the Narmer Palette (made around 3000 BC) shows the king wearing the White Crown of Upper Egypt on one side (shown here), and the Red Crown of Lower Egypt on the other. We assume that this iconography indicates that Egypt was either united before or during King Narmer's reign.

step pyramid at Meidum, south of Memphis, into the 'true' straight-sided pyramid we think of today, probably collapsed in antiquity.

The second of Seneferu's pyramids, however, was always intended to be built with smooth sides and edges – presumably representing the sun's rays descending to Earth rather than a stairway to heaven. In the course of this experimental work, however, a major settling of the interior of the structure forced the builders to lessen the angle at the top of the pyramid, producing the odd visual effect of the 'Bent Pyramid' at Dahshur.

Perhaps fearing that such a structure might not prove a fit place to spend eternity, Seneferu began a new pyramid a few kilometres to the north, and, in this 'Red' Pyramid (standing 104m/340ft high), he was finally buried far below a gilded capstone.

THE GREAT PYRAMID

Seneferu's son, Khufu (2589–2566 BC), known also by the Greek name 'Cheops', was to surpass his father by building the greatest pyramid of all – *Akhet-Khufu*, 'Horizon of Khufu' – on the Giza Plateau opposite modern Cairo.

The Great Pyramid, which was built over a 20-year period, was constructed of 2.3 million stone blocks averaging 2.5 tons each, most of which were quarried nearby. The outer smooth casing, however, was made from the finest Tura limestone from quarries across the Nile.

Standing 147m (482ft) high, the Great Pyramid would not be surpassed in height until the building of Lincoln Cathedral in England around 1300. Here the king was intended to rest for eternity protected by multiple complex architectural features, including a concealed entrance and massive granite blocks intended to stop tomb raiders.

Provided for Khufu's final river journey to his burial place, and for the travel of his soul in the company of the sun god Re, two extraordinary 43m (140ft) wooden boats were also buried beside the pyramid, which were interred after the Great Pyramid was sealed.

Khufu's final journey on land had also involved a vast complex of buildings. From a valley temple beside the Nile where his body was mummified, his coffin was dragged along a 825m (2700ft) polished stone causeway to a funerary temple and then on to his resting place.

In addition, to the east of the Great Pyramid three small pyramids were built for three of Khufu's queens (possibly one of these was built for Khufu's mother, Hetepheres, although the objects from her tomb were found elsewhere).

All these structures were mostly created by a year-round team of 4000 permanent workers – not slaves – who lived nearby in a settlement, *Gerget Khufu* ('Settlement of Khufu') composed of houses for managers and barracks for the workers. The dining halls of the settlement were supplied by nearby warehouses with bread, beer, fish and meat throughout the year. The small tombs of some of the workers are still there, benefiting in the afterlife from their proximity to the reborn king.

After a short interlude, King Khaefre (2558–2532 BC), a son of Khufu, returned to the site close to his father's pyramid at Giza. As, presumably, a dutiful son, he appears to have decided that his pyramid ('Khaefre is Great') should not be as tall as his father's so it is 2m

OPPOSITE:
Mastaba of Seshemnefer IV, Giza Plateau
Seen here in a fully developed form in front of the Great Pyramid (dating to the Sixth Dynasty, around 2340 BC), the low, rectangular tombs of nobles, known as mastabas, represented the first phase in the development of what we think of today as an ancient Egyptian pyramid.

(6ft) shorter. However, it was built on slightly higher ground, which causes to this day – as was no doubt intended in antiquity – some confusion concerning the identity of the Great Pyramid.

THE GREAT SPHINX

It was Khaefre who immortally and indelibly changed the landscape of the Giza Plateau by having sculptors transform a rock outcrop closer to the river into the body of a crouching lion crowned by a representation of his own regal head. Standing 20m (65ft) high and 70m (230ft) long, the idea of the Great Sphinx may have been the invention of the dowager queen Hetepheres II, who had such a sculpture created with her own face at Abu Rawash to the north.

The Great Sphinx is accompanied by the Sphinx Temple and the red granite Valley Temple that contained 24 fine statues of the king wearing the *nemes* headcloth with the goddess Wadjet at the front, and the wings of the falcon god Horus to the rear.

The third major pyramid at Giza was built by Khaefre's son Menkaure, and although the smallest of the three, the first 16 courses of the temple were, remarkably, made of granite, not the more easily worked limestone used by his father and grandfather. Menkaure appears to have died before the work was finished in the grander material, and the pyramid was completed in limestone. Menkaure's Valley Temple incorporated a spectacular series of statues of the king, the goddess Hathor and a representative of each of the 42 administrative areas of the country.

Menkaure's successors of the Fifth Dynasty (2494–2345 BC) built a similar great complex to the one at Giza at Abusir – including temples to the sun, supposedly just within sight of the golden tip of the obelisk of the great sun temple complex at Heliopolis to the north and across the river.

The last king of the Fifth Dynasty, Unas (2375–2345 BC), returned for burial at Saqqara. Although the outside of his pyramid appears as not much more than a pile of rubble, the interior walls of his burial chamber are covered with over 700 spells, prayers and hymns known as the 'Pyramid Texts'. These religious texts were considered so potent that hieroglyphs of dangerous beasts, such as lions or snakes, were carved in two halves, so that they could not reanimate in the netherworld and bring harm.

The Old Kingdom, the first great era of art and architecture in Egyptian history, came to an end amid challenges for power between the king and the priests of the sun god, and a period of decreased levels of the flooding of the Nile that had disastrous consequences both for the people and for the treasury of the state.

Surprisingly, the penultimate king of the Sixth Dynasty (the last of the Old Kingdom), Pepi II (2278–2184 BC), may have reigned for as many as 94 or 64 years – in either case an extraordinary length of time in antiquity. Under the circumstances afflicting the kingdom, however, his outliving of many possibly able successors may have dealt the final blow to order. Pepi II was succeeded briefly by one of his elderly sons, Nemtyemsaf II, but by then Egypt was slipping into civil war.

OPPOSITE:
Step Pyramid of Djoser, Saqqara
Designed by the great architect Imhotep, the Step Pyramid at Saqqara started as a large *mastaba* upon which additional layers of decreasing size were added – perhaps, simply, so that the structure could be seen more clearly from the capital city, Memphis, in the valley below. It is possible that the structure was always planned in this stepped form rather than being the accidental development usually described.

OPPOSITE:
Tiles in the form of reeds, Djoser Complex, Saqqara
Attached to the Step Pyramid was a large complex of buildings – including a palace and temples – that are thought to mimic in stone the structures Djoser would have known in life in Memphis. These would have been constructed of mud-brick, timber and reed matting; but, here, faience tiles and plaster represent the palace walls.

ABOVE:
Wadjet wall, Djoser Complex, Saqqara
In another part of Djoser's funerary complex, the goddess Wadjet – in the form of a rearing cobra, intimately linked to kingship and Lower Egypt – looks down protectively from the top of the walls. This representation of Wadjet formed part of the *uraeus*, at the front of the pharaoh's headdress.

OPPOSITE:
Seneferu's Pyramid, Meidum
Ancient Egypt's most prolific pyramid builder was King Seneferu (2613–2589 BC). Three large pyramids were constructed for his own burial alone. The first of these, at Meidum, was a step pyramid (perhaps begun by his predecessor), in which the steps were filled with limestone to produce four smooth sides. This extension, and other changes, reduced the integrity of the whole structure; at some point, most of the casing limestone slipped from the building.

ABOVE:
Rahotep and Nofret, Mastaba of Rahotep, Meidum
To be found in the Egyptian Museum in Cairo, the statues of Prince Rahotep and Nofret, probably from earlier in the reign of Seneferu, are bound by the strict conventional rules of Egyptian art of the period, yet still portray something of the character of the husband and wife.

FOLLOWING PAGES:
Meidum Geese, Meidum
A masterpiece of Ancient Egyptian art, the geese, which again can be found in the Egyptian Museum, Cairo, were painted on the plaster of the *mastaba* of Prince Nefermaat I, a son of Seneferu. Three geese face in either direction – the number three implying many birds. The depiction of the different plumage patterns of the geese reveal this to be the work of a master artist.

26

27

RIGHT:
Bent Pyramid, Dahshur
The second of Seneferu's pyramids was designed to be a true pyramid rather than having a step pyramid at its core. The lower part rises at an angle of 54 degrees to 47m (154ft), and then changes to a 43-degree angle, perhaps because of construction problems. This shallower angle was used for the 'Red Pyramid' – the first true pyramid, coated in smooth Tura limestone, and 1km (0.6 miles) north of the Bent Pyramid – where Seneferu was laid to rest.

FOLLOWING PAGES:
Pyramids at Giza
Already ancient by the time Classical Greece flourished, the pyramids at Giza represent the most iconic ancient Egyptian structures to have survived. The Great Pyramid of Khufu (right) is often mistaken for the slightly shorter pyramid of Khaefre that lies on higher ground. Three small 'satellite' pyramids are associated with Menkaure's pyramid (left).

Great Pyramid of Khufu, Giza Plateau

The Great Pyramid was built over a period of about 20 years as the tomb of King Khufu. It originally stood 147m (428ft) high, and each side measured 230m (750ft) at the base. The sides were composed of smooth limestone – some of this can still be seen around the base. There are at least three chambers within, including the burial chamber itself. A capstone (*pyramidion*) covered in gold or electrum would have completed the structure.

LEFT:
Solar Boat of Khufu, Giza Plateau
The solar boat on display at the Khufu Boat Museum is 43m (141ft) long, 6m (20ft) wide, and made of Lebanon cedar. This boat (one of two) was discovered in 1224 neatly-arranged pieces. It was probably used to ferry the body of the dead king from Memphis to Giza, but it would also have served the ritual purpose of being the means by which the risen king would travel across the heavens with the sun god Re.

FOLLOWING PAGES:
Queens' Pyramids, Great Pyramid, Giza Plateau
Three small pyramids lie in a row close to the eastern side of the Great Pyramid, and are assumed to have been the tombs of Khufu's senior wives. It is also possible that the largest of these was built for Khufu's mother, Hetepheres I, though her grave goods were found in a burial shaft 28m (92ft) to the east.

Grave Goods of Queen Hetepheres, Giza Plateau
Queen Hetepheres I was the wife of Seneferu and seemingly much-venerated mother of Khufu. Her well-constructed bed, canopy, armchairs and sedan chair can be seen in the Egyptian Museum, Cairo. Ancient Egyptian beds had a footboard, but no headboard, and this example was covered in gold leaf on four sides. The headrest was stored in a separate gold box.

Pyramid of Khaefre, Giza
Due to a rise in the bedrock, the base of Khaefre's pyramid is about 10m (33ft) higher than that of the Great Pyramid, giving the impression that it is a taller structure. It was originally 144m (470ft) high and 215m (705ft) wide at the base. Although at various times the smooth casing stones were carried away, they still remain at the top – giving an impression of how all the pyramids would have looked when constructed.

BOTH PAGES:
Statue of Khaefre, Lower Temple, Giza Plateau
Now to be seen in the Egyptian Museum in Cairo, Khaefre's statue – originally one of many within the Valley Temple on the river – is regarded as a supreme example of artistic skill in representing the king as both all-powerful and divine. The high degree of polishing across all the surfaces would have reflected the available light, and the green veins within the diorite stone would have enhanced the unworldly effect.

Great Sphinx, Giza Plateau
Generally believed to have been carved from the bedrock for Khaefre, the Great Sphinx – the king's head on a lion's body – measures 73m (240ft) from paw to tail, rises 20m (65ft) high, and is about 19m (62ft) wide across the haunches. The lower part of the sphinx is composed of softer limestone than the head; this led to a greater degree of erosion, which was repaired first in antiquity.

Pyramid of Menkaure, Giza Plateau
Originally 65m (213ft) high and approximately 103m (337ft) wide at the base, the pyramid of Khaefre's son, Menkaure, is the smallest of the main Giza pyramids. Remarkably, the first 16 courses of the pyramid are made of red granite, not the more easily worked local limestone, which was only used to complete the pyramid – presumably due to the king's unexpected death.

OPPOSITE:
Triad of Menkaure, Valley Temple, Giza
This is one of several triads found in the Valley Temple of Menkaure carved from single pieces of grey-green schist. Menkaure steps confidently forward in front of the goddess Hathor (wearing cow horns and a solar disk), and a personification of one of the administrative areas (or *nomes*) of Upper Egypt. (Egyptian Museum, Cairo.)

TOP:
Causeway and Pyramid of Unas, Saqqara
Unas (2375–2345 BC) was the last of the kings of the Fifth Dynasty, and reigned during a period of economic decline within Egypt. He was buried at Saqqara, where his pyramid can still be seen, though it is largely ruined (far distance). A 750m-long (2460-ft) causeway, carved with fine reliefs, connected the Valley Temple to a temple beside the pyramid.

ABOVE:
Detail of the Pyramid Texts, Pyramid of Unas, Saqqara
Unas was the first king to have the Pyramid Texts carved within his burial chamber and associated chambers – a ritual that was to continue among kings to the end of the Old Kingdom. The 283 'utterances' (or spells) were intended to assist the king in combatting hostile forces that might otherwise prevent him from joining with the sun god Re.

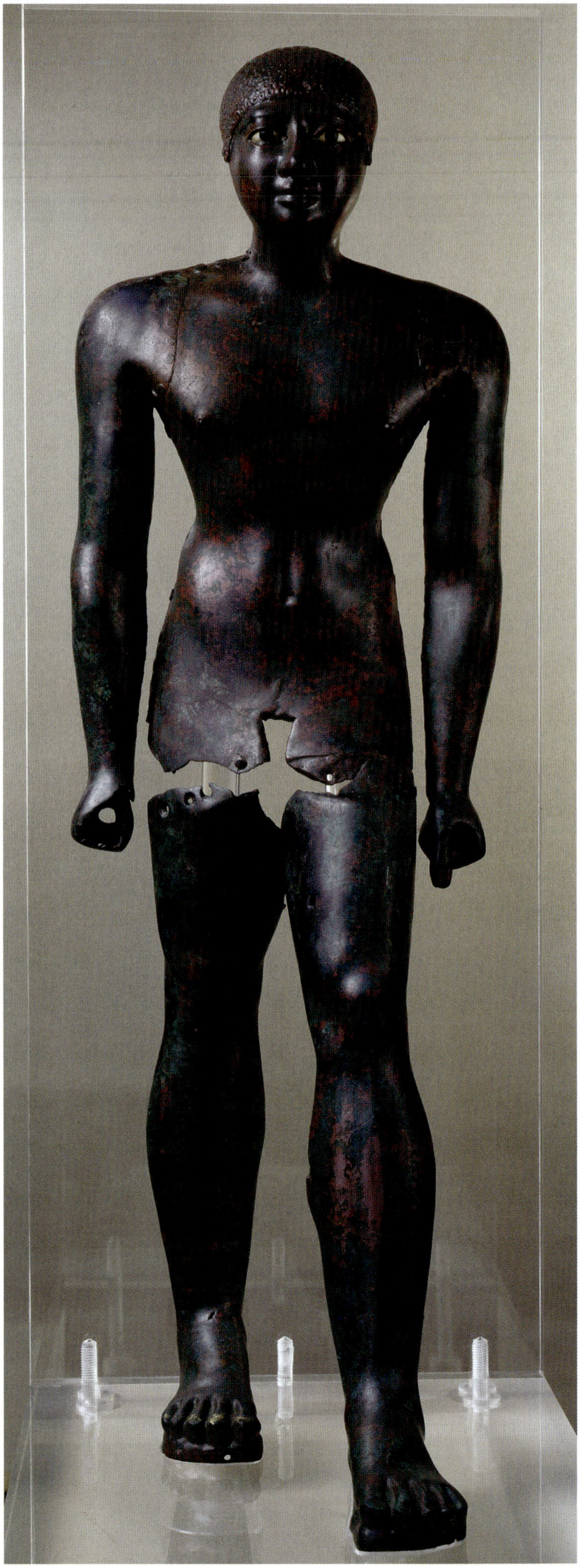

ABOVE:
Face of Ka-Aper, Mastaba of Ka-Aper, Saqqara
Old Kingdom artists were quite capable of producing naturalistic art, as in this Fifth Dynasty masterpiece of the priest Ka-Aper now in the Egyptian Museum, Cairo. The body is made of sycamore, which would have been lightly plastered and painted. The eyes are made from Egyptian alabaster, crystal, black stone and copper. The overall effect is, unmistakably, of a man fully content with his position in society.

RIGHT:
Statue of Merenra, Temple of Horus, Hierakonpolis
A technical tour-de-force, this life-size statue, usually thought to be of King Merenra (2287–2278 BC), was found together with a similar statue of his father Pepi I (2321–2287 BC). Made from beaten copper (originally) over a wooden frame, parts of the statue were covered in gold foil, and the eyes were created from limestone and obsidian.

OPPOSITE:
Tomb of Mereruka, Saqqara
Mereruka served the Sixth Dynasty King Teti (2345–2323 BC) as vizier. His power within the kingdom is reflected in his mastaba tomb at Saqqara, which contains 33 chambers. Here, Mereruka steps out from the netherworld to accept the offerings placed on the altar in front of him.

The Middle Kingdom

Within a few years of the death of Nemtyemsaf II, Egypt had descended into disorder and lawlessness – even the royal tombs were no longer safe from robbery.

The 14 or 15 kings recorded for the combined Seventh and Eighth Dynasties (between about 2181 and 2125 BC) suggest that the role was not a path to a long and happy life – only one king, Ibi, is known to have built a pyramid during this time.

Memphis declined in importance as warlords battled with each other or formed temporary alliances based on the old administrative areas (or *nomes*) – particularly in the south. Without central funding, the artistic output of the First Intermediate Period (2181–2055 BC) was largely limited to what a war lord or noble could still afford. Small 'states' emerged during this period, including the kingdom centred on Herakleopolis, just 90km (56 miles) south of Memphis, and another state around the hitherto minor town of Thebes (modern Luxor).

It was Thebes that gradually came to predominate during the Ninth and Tenth Dynasties (2160–2125 BC) – although often against formidable opposition – and about 2125 BC the Theban rulers became kings and gradually absorbed areas to the north, while maintaining a shaky truce with Herakleopolis.

When the Herakleopolitans finally made the mistake of breaking the truce during the reign of the Theban king Montjuhotep II (2055–2004 BC), his armies moved steadily north, eventually taking Herakleopolis itself, and, by doing so, reuniting Egypt.

Greatly respected for his achievement in ancient times, modern historians also regard Montjuhotep as laying the foundations of the Middle Kingdom (1985–1650 BC).

OPPOSITE:
Memorial Temple of Montjuhotep II (foreground), Deir el-Bahari
The Theban Montjuhotep II (2055–2004 BC) is credited with reuniting Egypt after the chaotic First Intermediate Period. His memorial temple (foreground), overshadowed today by the temple of Hatshepsut (in the process of reconstruction here), consisted of a forecourt (right), a ramp and a terrace of 80 columns surrounding a pyramid or mound, with a long (150m/490ft) passageway leading to the burial chamber beneath the cliffs.

Securely established, Montjuhotep II began to build at Dendera and Thebes, but his greatest building project was his own funerary complex at Deir el-Bahari (although, today, the remains of his temple are dwarfed by the later memorial temple of the female king, Hatshepsut).

Montjuhotep's temple was approached by a 46m (150ft) causeway that opened out into a forecourt of flowers and trees. A central ramp then rose to a terrace containing a virtual forest of 80 pillars surrounding a square structure that may well have been a pyramid (or a mound). Within a further courtyard closer to the cliff lay the beginning of a 150m (490ft) passage stretching under the base of the cliffs sacred to the goddess Hathor.

THE MIDDLE KINGDOM FLOURISHES

Montjuhotep II was succeeded by two other kings bearing that name, and upon the death of Montjuhotep IV, his first minister Amenemhat appears to have seized the throne and inaugurated the Twelfth Dynasty as Amenemhat I (reigned 1985–1955 BC).

Amenemhat – specifically ignoring the political history associated with Memphis – created a new capital of the reunited Egypt (*Itjtawy* – 'Seizer of the Two Lands', near modern Lisht) within the Fayoum – the extensive, fertile lake area to the west of the Nile Valley. He also established a new royal cemetery nearby, which relied heavily on stone transferred from the older, but now damaged, buildings at Giza, Saqqara and Dahshur.

Increasingly secure within Egypt, Amenemhat greatly strengthened the borders of Egypt with forts – particularly to the northeast facing southwest Asia; to the south, securing access to the gold routes of Nubia; and to the west against the tribes in what would become Libya.

Simultaneously, he weakened the power of the formerly unruly *nomes* by replacing their leaders with his supporters. The nomes remained centres of both power and wealth, however, which is best illustrated by the beautiful (slightly later) tombs from the nome centred on Beni Hasan in the middle of Egypt.

Crucially and highly unusually, in order to make the succession crystal-clear, Amenemhat made his son Senwosret co-ruler around the 20th year of his reign. It was just as well, as shortly before his 30th year on the throne, Amenemhat was assassinated by his own bodyguard. Whatever the circumstances behind that event, his son seems to have established his authority quickly and buried his father at Lisht.

During his own long reign, Senwosret I (1965–1921 BC) firmly established an Egyptian presence in Nubia and, less substantially, but perhaps more ruthlessly, in Palestine. At home, he built extensively in honour of the gods: at Heliopolis to the sun god Re; at Shedet (in the Fayoum) to the crocodile god Sobek; at Koptos to the fertility god Min; and on Elephantine Island (Aswan) to the river goddess Satis. At Thebes, he built shrines associated with a number of gods, and his magnificent White Chapel can still be seen in the open-air museum at Karnak. For himself, finally, he constructed his own pyramid and smaller pyramids for members of the royal family at Lisht.

OPPOSITE:

Colossal Statue of Montjuhotep II, Deir el-Bahari
To be seen today in the Egyptian Museum, Cairo, this colossal statue formed part of the burial chamber of the dead king. Montjuhotep wears the red crown of Lower Egypt and the white cloak associated with the jubilees of the king's reign. The body of the king is painted black, probably as an allusion to the god of the afterlife, Osiris. The false beard is curved – indicating the divine status of the deceased king.

Senwosret's immediate successors reigned in a period of stability and fruitfulness, interspersed with military action in Palestine and Syria. This action was counterbalanced to some degree by the peaceful settling of traders and artisans from Palestine in the eastern part of the Delta. Senwosret II (1880–1874 BC) created a new burial complex at Lahun in the Fayoum from which many spectacular objects were retrieved during excavations beginning in the late 1880s.

The surviving statues of his son, Senwosret III (1874–1855 BC), are remarkable for their naturalistic style and the possibility that they may be true portraits – with their characteristic careworn lines and heavy eyelids. Nevertheless, it appears that Senwosret III was not a popular figure in Egypt – all of the statues of him were vandalized shortly after his death. The source of this apparent enmity is not entirely clear. Possibly, it was because he greatly increased the state's central bureaucracy at the expense of the provincial governors, therefore arousing their jealousy and ultimate revenge.

He also waged a series of brutal wars against Nubia, which completed the subjugation of the northern part of the region, and, in the other direction, fought his way northeast beyond where Jerusalem now stands. Senwosret III's stern-faced statues were planted wherever he went, and his ultimate perception of his self-worth (which may also have been the source of enmity) is illustrated by the large memorial complex he had built at Abydos close to the Temple of Osiris and among the tombs of the first great kings of Egypt.

As his father had done before him, Senwosret III established his succession by drawing in his son as a co-regent long before his death. Amenemhat III (1855–1808 BC) seems to have followed his father's military inclinations, but also continued to place a particular emphasis on reclaiming agricultural land in the Fayoum and contributing to its temples (and to the temple of the cat goddess Bastet at Bubastis in the Delta). He was buried at a new site in the Fayoum, Hawara, where the accompanying memorial buildings were so complex that they became immortalized in the ancient world as 'The Labyrinth'.

THE MIDDLE KINGDOM DECLINES

The Twelfth Dynasty ended quite soon after the death of Amenemhat III, and, as if exhausted by another period of 'greatness', Egypt entered into one of its recurrent prolonged periods of fractured rule.

It was not, though, a period of particularly rapid decline – the Thirteenth Dynasty lasted between 1795 and 1650 BC – but it was characterized by up to 70 rulers, some of whom were commoners elevated to kingship. Towards the end of this period, Egypt appears to have disintegrated into a number of local kingdoms (in particular, dividing again into north and south – a Fourteenth Dynasty between 1750 and 1650 BC coexisted for a time with the remnants of the Thirteenth Dynasty), and the state had lost much of its influence or control over areas in the Levant and Nubia, where a new independent kingdom emerged.

These circumstances gave ample opportunity for the takeover of much of the Egyptian state by an enigmatic foreign group of 'Palestinian' origin, known as the Hyksos.

OPPOSITE:
Clapping Women, Tomb of Neferu, Deir el-Bahari
Dating from the reign of Montjuhotep II, this relief from the tomb of his wife Neferu illustrates the importance of music and dance in religious rituals, especially associated with the goddess of femininity, Hathor. The performers are dressed in long high-waisted skirts and wear a row of large (probably) silver beads in their hair. (Cincinnati Art Museum.)

PREVIOUS PAGES:

Stela of Abkau (detail), Abydos
In this superbly carved Eleventh Dynasty limestone block, the deceased Overseer of Herds Abkau, and his wife Imemi, sit in front of a large funerary meal. Family members and household staff also bring gifts that will be useful in the afterlife. To the immediate left of Abkau, a servant is bent over by the weight of the cow's leg he is offering, and below him another servant respectfully pours libations for the couple.

BELOW:

Forty Nubian Archers, Tomb of Mesheti, Asyut
An effective illustration of the nature of the First Intermediate Period and the early years of the Middle Kingdom, the nome governor Mesheti sought to be protected in death by soldiers – including the much-feared Nubian bowmen and Egyptian spearmen. (Egyptian Museum, Cairo.)

ABOVE:

Amenemhat I, Pyramid Complex, Lisht North

Now to be seen in the Metropolitan Museum, New York, the lintel, from which this detail is taken, is one of the finest objects to have survived from Amenemhat's reign (1985–1955 BC). The king holds the *nekhakha* flail – a symbol associated with the god Osiris and the fertility of the land – in his right hand.

LEFT:
Woman Carrying Basket, Tomb of Meketre, Deir el-Bahari
Probably dating to the early reign of Amenemhat I, this delightful figure was found in the tomb of the Chief Steward Meketre, alongside a number of models intended to work for the deceased in the afterlife. The feather pattern on the dress on this statue (and its partner) suggest an additional divine aspect to the figure. Perhaps, the pair also represent the goddesses Isis and Nephthys – protectors of the dead.

OPPOSITE:
Model of a Livestock Census, Tomb of Meketre, Deir el-Bahari
Crafted by a great artist who captured perfectly the liveliness of the scene, Meketre, accompanied by a son and four scribes, watches on while cattle are driven forward to be counted. Each figure has a role to play in the scene – ensuring an efficient census. (Egyptian Museum, Cairo.)

ABOVE:
Model of a Granary with Scribes, Tomb of Meketre, Deir el-Bahari
This scene emphasizes the vital importance of wheat and barley to the Egyptian economy. All towns and villages would have had granary facilities, as represented here (to be seen in the Metropolitan Museum, New York), from which people would draw rations and wages. Four scribes sit in a room behind the entrance door, carefully noting the arrival of each sack before workers climb the stairs to pour the grain into silos.

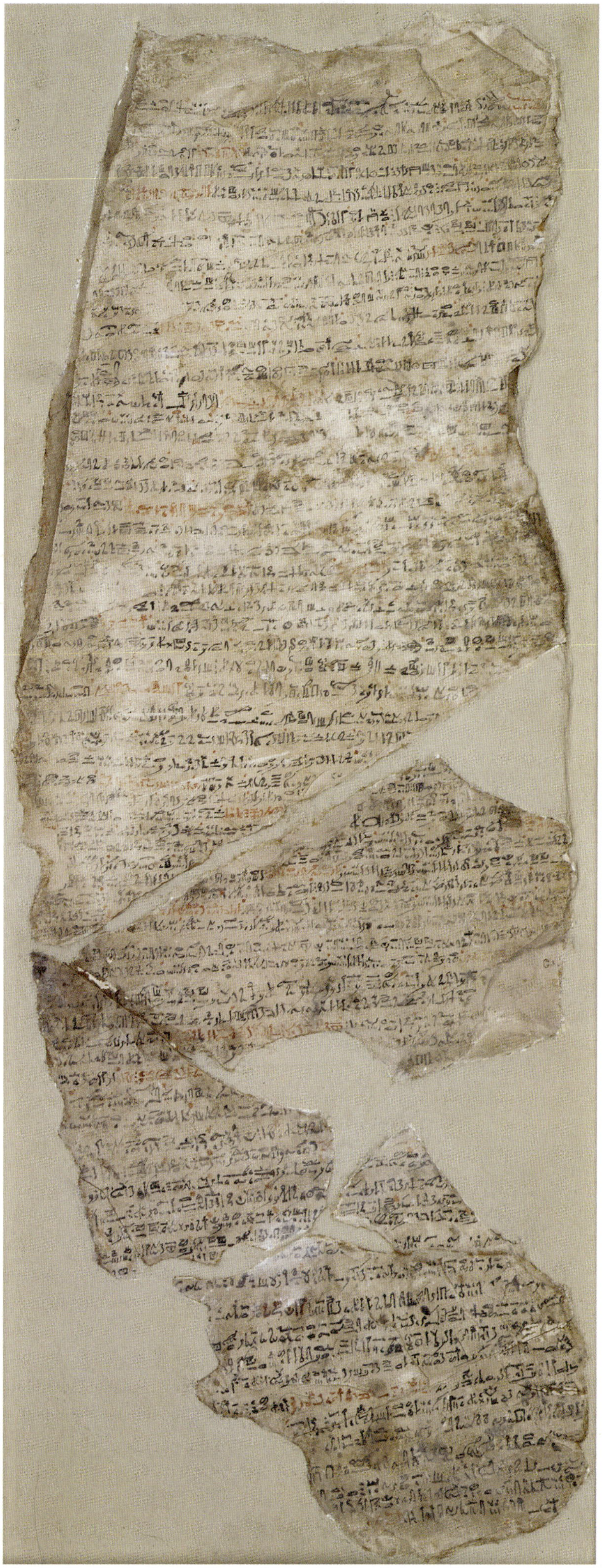

LEFT:
The Tale of Sinuhe
Seen here in a New Kingdom copy (Nineteenth Dynasty, 1295–1186 BC) housed in the Ashmolean Museum, Oxford, *The Tale of Sinuhe* is a masterpiece of ancient Egyptian poetry. The 575 verses are set in the period after the death of Amenemhat I and tell the story of Sinuhe, who flees from Egypt to the Levant after overhearing a conspiracy against the king. He settles in his new home, but as an old man he longs to return to Egypt. He is invited to return to his beloved homeland by Senwosret I, and is laid to rest in a beautiful tomb.

LEFT:
Obelisk of Senwosret I, Heliopolis
Remarkably, the obelisk erected by Senwosret I at the temple of Re-Atum in ancient Heliopolis still stands in its original position within a suburb of modern Cairo. The red granite obelisk is 21m (69ft) high, and weighs 120 tons.

OPPOSITE:
The Face of Senwosret I, Temple of Amun-Re, Karnak
This young, smiling face is part of a colossal statue of the king now in the Medelhavsmuseet, Stockholm. The statue, in the form of a shrouded or mummy-like figure, was part of a group that flanked the entrance to the great temple holding the *ankh* symbol of life.

OPPOSITE:

White Chapel of Senwosret I, Karnak

Magnificently carved, the limestone jubilee chapel of Senwosret can be seen today in the Open Air Museum at Karnak Temple. The pieces of the chapel were found in 1927 serving as rubble inside the New Kingdom third pylon (gate) of the Temple of Amun-Re. Within the reliefs the king is crowned and honoured by the gods Amun, Min, Horus and Ptah.

ABOVE:

A Queen or Princess as a Sphinx, Twelfth Dynasty

Delicately carved and immediately arresting, this head was found near Rome and may have belonged to the Emperor Hadrian, but is now in the Brooklyn Museum. It formed part of a sphinx and probably dates to the reign of Senwosret II (1880–1874 BC). The eyes would have been inlaid, and it is likely that the head was damaged as they were removed.

OPPOSITE:
Diadem of Princess Sithathoryunet, Senwosret II Complex, Lahun
Made principally of gold, lapis lazuli and carnelian, this exquisite diadem was found hidden in the wall of the princess' tomb at Lahun, and was intended to be worn over a wig. At the front of the band – decorated with rosettes – there is a striking cobra *uraeus* as a symbol of the princess' royal status, and, at the rear, two plumes rise indicating her royal/divine nature. Ornamental ribbons of gold fall down from the band. (Egyptian Museum, Cairo.)

ABOVE:
Girdle, anklets and bracelets of Princess Sithathoryunet, Lahun
The girdle is composed of golden feline heads linked by amethyst beads, the anklets are clawed, and the bracelets contain a resting lion, in this spectacular set of jewellery. Presumably worn ceremonially, the imagery suggests the lioness goddesses associated with the 'Eye of Re' who protected the sun god on his daily journey across the sky. (Metropolitan Museum of Art, New York.)

RIGHT:
Cosmetic jar of Princess Sithathoryunet, Lahun
Made of obsidian (probably from Ethiopia) and gold, this royal kohl jar serves as a reminder of the important part that cosmetics played in the lives of both men and women. Kohl was made from powdering minerals including galena (black) and malachite (green) and applied around the eyes.

ABOVE:

Hunting Wildfowl (detail), Tomb of Khnumhotep II, Beni Hasan
This rich scene, from the tomb of a nomarch of an Upper Egyptian administrative area, provides evidence for the continuing power of the *nomes*, even as that was being increasingly reined in by the Middle Kingdom kings. Here, in the afterlife, Khnumhotep is engaged in netting large numbers of waterfowl.

OPPOSITE:

Khnumhotep II, East Wall, Tomb of Khnumhotep II, Beni Hasan
The east wall of Khnumhotep II's tomb contains two large images of the nomarch hunting: one in which he is using a harpoon to spear fish, and this image of him using a throwing stick to bring down waterfowl. Scenes such as these reflect the continuing power of the deceased to maintain order, and his eternal renewal.

ABOVE:

The Aamu, Tomb of Khnumhotep II, Beni Hasan
The distant trading links of the richer *nomes* is attested by this scene of traders from far-off southwest Asia – identified here as *Aamu* – bringing offerings of exotic animals to the deceased nomarch. It is sometimes said that these people may have been ancestors of the Hyksos, who were later to take control of northern Egypt.

OPPOSITE:

Face of Senwosret III
Traditionally, the kings of ancient Egypt were portrayed as muscular young men, who either gently smiled at their subjects or looked suitably sombre. Portraits of Senwosret III, however, depart from this model by showing the king as an authoritative, older, thoughtful man, taking his responsibilities as king – as intermediary between the gods and the people – fully upon his shoulders. (Metropolitan Museum of Art, New York.)

ABOVE:

Necklace and pectoral of Senwosret III, Funerary Complex, Dahshur

Found hidden in the tomb of Princess Mereret, this pectoral may have been a gift from her father Senwosret III (ruled 1878–1839 BC). Delicately framed by the walls of a sanctuary, the goddess Nekhbet – patron of southern Egypt – appears above, spreading her wings protectively, and holding two *shen* signs of protection. Below, two falcon-headed sphinxes attack the enemies of Egypt. (Egyptian Museum, Cairo.)

RIGHT:

Amenemhat III wearing the White Crown
This head is so magnificently carved (in graywacke) by a master craftsman it is hard to believe that this not an actual portrait of the king. As is true of most ancient Egyptian sculptures, this head would have been painted, and the image of a thoughtful, mature king – worn down to a degree by the affairs of state – must have been highly effective royal propaganda.

ABOVE:

Pectoral of Amenemhat III, Pyramid Complex, Dahshur

The pectoral bears the name of Amenemhat III and was also found in the tomb of Princess Mereret (a daughter of Senwosret III) at Dahshur. The gold, carnelian, lapis lazuli and faience pectoral shows a scene beloved of all pharaohs – the smiting of foreign enemies. Above, the vulture goddess Nekhbet spreads her wings protectively. (Egyptian Museum, Cairo.)

OPPOSITE:

***Ka* Statue of Hor, Dahshur**

This delicate wooden statue of a Thirteenth Dynasty (1795–1650 BC) king (in the Egyptian Museum, Cairo), represents the vital force or *ka* of the deceased (identified by the hieroglyphic sign on the head), before which offerings would be made by mourners or priests of the memorial cult. The radiant life force of the king is emphasized by the rock crystal and bronze inlaid eyes.

The New Kingdom

The origins of the most golden of the golden ages of Egypt – the New Kingdom (around 1550–1069 BC) – were particularly inauspicious. Although people of Palestinian origin ('Aamu' or 'Asiatics') had been established in communities in the Delta for generations, around 1650 BC a group of princes (the Fifteenth Dynasty, 1650–1550 BC) took control of large swathes of Egyptian territory – at least down to Hermopolis (south of modern Minya) – from Avaris, their capital in the Delta. This left only a rump native state centered on Thebes (the Sixteenth and Seventeenth Dynasties). Thebes, in turn, was threatened from the south by a new Nubian state allied with the Hyksos to the north.

OPPOSITE:
Fly Pendant Necklace, Tomb of Queen Ahhotep II, Dra' Abu el-Naga'
Queen Ahhotep II was probably the Great Wife of Kamose (1555–1500), and appears to have been personally involved in the expulsion of the Hyksos – unusually, her tomb on the West Bank at Luxor contained ceremonial weapons. This gold fly pendant necklace, in the Luxor Museum, is also of a form that was presented by the king to soldiers who showed conspicuous valour on the battlefield.

Although the Hyksos of this Second Intermediate Period (1650–1550 BC) were characterized by later Egyptians as brutish and uncivilized invaders, it is clear that although they continued to maintain some Palestinian customs, they were thoroughly acclimatized to Egyptian traditions and practices. In addition, their origins and extensive trading partnerships facilitated the introduction of new technologies – including the composite bow, the *khopesh* curved sword and, above all, the lightweight, highly manoeuvrable chariot – that were, ironically, to play a part in the later expulsion of the Hyksos from Egypt and provide the underpinning for the subsequent resurgence of the Egyptian Empire.

By adopting these technologies during the course of constant warfare, and through an apparently inextinguishable belief in its own legitimacy, the Theban state survived under its kings (including the formidable regent queen mother, Ahhotep). In this spirit, the Theban king Kamose (around 1555–1550 BC) seems to have hardly hesitated to attack both the Hyksos and Nubia 'to save Egypt'.

Having subdued Nubia, Kamose turned north and pressed on almost to the gates of Avaris. He was not able to take the city, however, and withdrew south – no doubt with considerable spoils of war that might underwrite a campaign the next year. It was a campaign that he would not see, however, for he died shortly after his return to Thebes.

EGYPT IS REUNITED (AGAIN)

Kamose's successor, Ahmose I (1550–1525 BC), seems to have been a boy at the time of his succession, but around 1540–1535 BC, after a prolonged siege, he forced the Hyksos princes from Avaris, out of Egypt, and on to the Palestinian fortress of Sharuhen, where they were again besieged, expelled and pursued deeper into Palestine and Syria. Nearer to home, parts of Nubia were also regained for the crown before the warrior king died in his 30s and was buried not far from the entrance to the Valley of the Kings.

These events inaugurated the period known to us as the New Kingdom (1550–1069 BC), beginning with the Eighteenth Dynasty (1550–1295 BC). The achievements of Ahmose I were consolidated by his son, Amenhotep I (1525–1504 BC), under the regency of his powerful mother Ahmes-Nefertiry, and a considerable amount of restoration work within Egypt was carried out during his reign.

Amenhotep I, who died in his 20s, may have been the first Egyptian king to be buried in a hidden tomb high up within the Valley of the Kings close to the natural pyramidal peak at its head, although this is uncertain. Apparently childless, Amenhotep I was succeeded by the warrior king Thutmose I (1504–1492 BC) who pushed the boundaries of the Egyptian empire to the Euphrates River to the northeast, and gained territory further south in Nubia – between the Fourth and Fifth Cataracts across the Nile.

Under Thutmose I, the former city of Avaris – now the royal quarters and military staging post of Perunefer – was expanded, and some of its buildings incorporated distinctly Minoan decoration, a clear indication of the expanded presence and alliances created by Egypt in the eastern Mediterranean. The king also added significantly to the temple of Karnak in the Theban homeland.

Upon his premature death, Thutmose I was buried in the Valley of the Kings. He was succeeded by Thutmose II (1492–1479 BC), whose Great Wife was Hatshepsut, a daughter of Thutmose I. Thutmose II was, in turn, succeeded by a young son, Thutmose III (1479–1425 BC), under the regency of his stepmother and aunt, Hatshepsut.

This pattern of a dowager queen regent exercising power in the name of a king who was not yet old enough to rule should, by now, be familiar to the reader, but Hatshepsut – perhaps building upon the very powerful positions of recent queens regent and recalling 'female kings' in the more distant past – declared herself to be king (1473–1458 BC) in about the seventh year of Thutmose III's reign. She can be seen portrayed with the crowns of Upper and Lower Egypt and the false beard of a 'pharaoh' (a word derived from an Egyptian term that arose at this time).

OPPOSITE:

Temple of Hatshepsut, Deir el-Bahari
Restored to something of its former glory, the temple of the female king Hatshepsut (1473–1458 BC) was designed by the architect Senenmut. There are three layered terraces of columns – the top colonnade fronted by statues of Hatshepsut in the form of the god Osiris – connected by long ramps. Deir el-Bahari was long associated with the goddess Hathor, for whom there is a chapel, but the principal focus of the temple was the rock-cut chapel to the god Amun of Karnak.

The 14-year relationship as co-rulers between Thutmose III – who was still nominally the principal king – and Hatshepsut was clearly complex. It seems to have largely settled down into Thutmose III waging war beyond Egypt's borders (in Palestine and Nubia), and Hatshepsut controlling affairs within those borders (although she was also famously responsible for the trading mission to the Land of 'Punt' depicted at her memorial temple).

THE MOST SACRED OF PLACES

When Hatshepsut died around 1458 BC, she was buried in the Valley of the Kings next to her father Thutmose I, but it is for her memorial temple (*Djeser-djeseru*, 'the most sacred of places', at Deir al-Bahari on the west bank opposite Luxor) that she and her architect Senenmut are most justly famous.

The new building came to dwarf the memorial temple of Montjuhotep II beside it. Hatshepsut's temple was approached by a processional way bordered by sphinxes, and the multi-layered front of the temple was a forest of columns and colossal statues of the ruler in the guise of the god Osiris.

The ultimate focus of the temple, however, was the shrine high up in the temple and cut into the cliff. It was here that the god Amun-Re of Karnak temple would rest each year during the annual procession of his image between the temples on the west bank of the Nile.

Some 20 years after the presumed death of Hatshepsut, Thutmose III attempted to remove all mentions of her name from monuments in Egypt. It seems a long period to hold a grudge, and we don't entirely understand its basis. At the great temple of Karnak across the river, Hatshepsut's obelisks were even surrounded by high walls so that no one could get close enough to read the texts.

THUTMOSE III GOES TO WAR

Now sole ruler, Thutmose III quickly established his lasting reputation as one of the great warrior kings of Egypt – particularly associated with the domination of the kingdoms within Palestine and Syria. In the 33 years of his reign, he crossed the Euphrates River – which had marked the limit of his grandfather Thutmose I's campaigns – and defeated the Mitanni, one of the major powers of the time. Further to the north, he reached and defeated the city of Carchemish and, later, the crossroads city of Qadesh. Such was his success in battle that the kings of Babylon and of the Hittites (within modern Turkey) thought it was good politics to send gifts and messages of peace to their brother king.

Importantly for the future of the Egyptian state, instead of imposing direct Egyptian rule over the conquered territories, Thutmose III preferred a policy whereby the kings of local city-states became client-kings – these kings having been brought up and educated in Egypt as children.

Towards the end of his reign, the king memorialized 20 years of fighting and the lands he had seen on the walls of Karnak temple, which he added to extensively (as he

OPPOSITE:
Soldiers from the Expedition to the Land of Punt, Temple of Hatshepsut
Partly to bring exotic plants to the 'garden for my father Amun' at Deir el-Bahari, Hatshepsut sent an armed trading expedition to the mysterious Land of Punt to the south (possibly an area including parts of modern Somalia, Ethiopia or eastern Sudan).

did to temples elsewhere) while also building a memorial temple for himself at Deir el-Bahari beside that of Hatshepsut.

After a reign of over 50 years, the great warrior and patron of the arts was buried in the Valley of the Kings by his son and successor Amenhotep II (reigned 1427–1400 BC) in a magnificent quartzite sarcophagus. Amenhotep II's reign was largely dominated by military expeditions in Syria in imitation of his father's career – although tempered by building at home and attempts to rebalance the growing power of the priesthood of Amun-Re at Karnak by supporting the northern priesthood at Heliopolis.

Another short reign followed (Thutmose IV, 1400–1390 BC), and again there are signs that the king sought to distance the throne from the power of the Karnak priests and their influence on the succession – not least by restoring the Great Sphinx (by now seen as representing an aspect of the sun god, Re, as Re-Horakhty).

Thutmose IV was succeeded by a young son, Amenhotep III (1390–1352 BC) under the regency of his mother, Mutemwia. The Egyptian kingdom that the 10-year-old inherited was not by this time only immensely rich, but also for the most part at peace. Together with his wife Tiy and his supremely able scribe Amenhotep son of Hapu, Amenhotep III developed into less of a warrior king, becoming instead the most prolific builder Egypt had yet seen. A royal residence was begun at Thebes on the west bank at Malqata (south of Medinet Habu), and the king spent increasing amounts of time there until, at last, it became his permanent home.

Across the river he built new monuments of great splendour at Karnak, including two obelisks between which the sun rose every morning; a new 'pylon' or gate; a new sacred boat on which the image of the god Amun could be carried; and a new shrine to Amun covered in a ton of lapis lazuli and five tons of gold.

LUXOR TEMPLE

A few kilometres to the south, Amenhotep added to the temple at Luxor through a delightful colonnade leading to a spacious court open to the sun, and beyond to rooms in which the king could be surrounded by images of his own divine birth. Simultaneously, however, he made preparations for his death, which occurred in the 39th year of his reign.

He was buried in the Western Valley of the Kings, and his memorial temple – the largest structure of its kind in Egyptian history – lay in front of the cliffs of the West Bank of the Nile. Relatively little of this memorial temple still stands – it was laid low by an earthquake in antiquity – yet the remaining colossal statues that stood before the gate still provide one of the most evocative images that has survived from ancient Egypt – the so-called 'Colossi of Memnon' (wrongly ascribed in antiquity to a mythical Greek hero).

Amenhotep III was succeeded by his son, Amenhotep IV (1352–1336 BC), better known to posterity as 'Akhenaten'.

The concept of the Aten, as the physical embodiment of the sun, had already enjoyed a long history, but, during the reign of

OPPOSITE:

Priests Carrying a Sacred Barque, Red Chapel of Hatshepsut, Karnak
The purpose of the rock-cut chapel at Hatshepsut's temple was to house the sacred barque (or boat) carrying the image of the god Amun-Re on its annual procession to the West Bank at Thebes during the 'Beautiful Festival of the Valley'. This image from the Red Chapel, which once stood in the centre of the sanctuary of Amun-Re and has been reconstructed in the Open Air Museum at Karnak, shows the priests carrying the sacred barque on its journey.

Amenhotep III, the Aten developed into a major deity equated to a large degree with the person of the king.

After a few years of ruling Egypt, Amenhotep IV elevated this concept to a greater height while still acknowledging the traditional gods and goddesses. Both the king and his consort, Nefertiti, became directly associated with the Aten – their 'otherness' as divine being perhaps explaining the extreme representations of the couple, with emaciated features, large paunches and swollen hips and breasts, characteristic of the period.

In pursuit of the worship of the Aten, Amenhotep IV established a new capital (Akhet-Aten, or 'Horizon of the Aten', which, as modern Amarna, gave its name to the 'Amarna Period') in the middle of the country, and changed his name to Akhenaten ('Incarnation of the Aten').

Within the bounds of Akhet-Aten, new palaces, offices and temples rapidly arose – including two great open sanctuaries dedicated entirely to Aten worship. In counterbalance, and perhaps as a final part of the political processes begun under Amenhotep II, Akhenaten closed the great temple of Karnak (where he had purposefully built a new temple to the Aten outside the precinct walls), and suppressed – with the aid of soldiers withdrawn from Egypt's border – the worship of Amun and his priesthood.

TUTANKHAMUN

In the 17th year of his reign Akhenaten died, was buried at Amarna, and was succeeded by his co-ruler, the female king Neferneferuaten (the former Nefertiti). The new king oversaw her husband's legacy for only a few years before succumbing herself. She was succeeded by their 10-year-old son, Tutankhaten.

With both Akhenaten and Nefertiti dead, Amarna was abandoned and the cult of Amun made a rapid resurgence – the young king changing his name to Tutankhamun (1336–1327 BC) and issuing a formal decree, 'seeking what was beneficial to his father Amun', and restoring the old temples and priesthood to their former status.

During his short reign, Tutankhamun contributed significantly to the temples at Luxor and Karnak, as well as Memphis, but it was in death that he was to become famous. He was still no more than a teenager when he died – the last member of Akhenaten's immediate family to rule Egypt. Although a tomb may have been started for him elsewhere in the Valley of the Kings, his sudden death meant that another burial site – on which work was more advanced – had to be appropriated for him.

It seems that every conceivable object – both valuable and utilitarian – associated with the young king was placed in the tomb with him. We do not know whether this was usual or if the recently reinstated priests of Amun took the opportunity to quickly bury all the remaining objects from the royal palaces associated with the reviled family of Akhenaten. Certainly, some of the 5,400 objects that were buried in the tomb were made for other members of his family, and there are repeated references to the Aten associated with the objects. We know this because,

OPPOSITE:
Obelisk of Hatshepsut, Karnak
During the period in which Thutmose III attempted to expunge the name of Hatshepsut, he ordered the destruction of the Red Chapel and the removal of her name and representation from Karnak temple. A curtain wall was also placed around two of the obelisks that Hatshepsut erected here, obscuring them from view. Ironically, this preserved them for posterity (the remains of the other obelisk are beside the Sacred Lake at Karnak).

miraculously, the tomb remained intact through the centuries.

Thieves had broken in a short time after the funeral, but the stolen items were quickly retrieved and the damage repaired. Not long after, nature intervened in the form of a flash flood that carried tons of debris into the valley, and deeply covered the entrance to the tomb.

There the king lay surrounded by what were to become some of the most familiar treasures to have survived from ancient Egypt – including the golden mask, the throne and the young man's hunting chariots – discovered by the British archaeologist Howard Carter in 1922.

Tutankhamun was succeeded briefly by an elderly soldier and probable relative, Ay (1327–1323 BC), who in turn was succeeded by another military man (fresh from fighting in Palestine), Horemheb (1323–1295 BC). He reigned long enough to begin the long process of righting the Egyptian ship of state after the tumultuous years, both at home and abroad, of the Amarna Period.

THE RAMESIDE KINGS

Horemheb reorganized both the army and the state's administrative apparatus before he nominated a military colleague, General Paramessu, as his successor. Horemheb removed the temple of the Aten from Karnak, using the material in his own construction work to the glory of Amun, and, similarly, continued his predecessors' building work at Luxor temple. He was buried in a magnificent tomb in the Valley of the Kings in a ceremony conducted by his nominated successor.

Unlike any king after Akhenaten, General Paramessu – as Rameses I (1295–1294 BC), the founder of the Nineteenth Dynasty – had the good fortune to already have children who could succeed him. It was just as well, for within two years Rameses I – having carried on the reforms initiated by his mentor – also died, allowing the succession of his son Seti I (1294–1279 BC).

The new pharaoh was a rare combination of military leader and connoisseur of the arts. In his first year as king, the Egyptian army pushed deep into Palestine and Syria, coming into direct conflict with the emerging power of the Hittites spreading southward from their homeland in Anatolia (now the eastern part of Turkey), especially around Qadesh on the Orontes River. Similar campaigns against tribes to the west of Egypt, and against Nubia, gradually increased the security of Egypt's borders.

At home, Seti I ordered the construction of some of the masterpieces of ancient Egyptian architecture, including the Osiris temple at Abydos, with its magnificent and delicate raised relief images of the king in the presence of gods and goddesses, and the majestic 134 columns of the Great Hypostyle Hall at Karnak. Perhaps his greatest achievement, however, was his tomb in the Valley of the Kings, where every wall was covered by a masterpiece painted below a ceiling composed of exquisitely rendered astronomical figures and gods.

Unusually in ancient Egyptian history, Seti I is sometimes depicted with his son, Prince Rameses, presumably in order to emphasize that there should be no question about the eventual succession. In due course,

OPPOSITE:

Statue of Thutmose III, Karnak Cachette
This magnificent greywacke statue of the great military pharaoh was found in 1904 in the courtyard of Karnak temple with many other statues that had been cleared from the temple by the priests. In keeping with royal propaganda, Thutmose appears eternally youthful. (Luxor Museum.)

his son ascended the throne as Rameses II (1279–1213 BC).

RAMESES II

Longevity was not an expected attribute in ancient Egypt, not even among kings, and from the moment of his accession Rameses II appears to have been a young man in a hurry. This is nowhere clearer than in the manner in which he completed his father's construction work at Abydos: the delicate raised relief (where the background behind the figures was carved away) of the inner temple was replaced by sunk relief (where the figures are carved into the flat background) in the outer temple – sunk relief was both quicker and easier to produce. The first pylon at Luxor, through which the temple is entered today, and the court behind, were similarly constructed within only a few years of Rameses II's reign.

Ultimately, the name of Rameses II was carved deeply into many new buildings, restored buildings, and practically every other structure throughout Egypt. Of particular importance, he built a new capital – Piramesses, 'the house of Rameses' – in the northeast of the Nile Delta on the site of the old Hyksos capital of Avaris (although little of this stands above ground today). To the south, within Lower Nubia, he built, completed or restored a number of temples, including the justly famous twin rock-carved temples at Abu Simbel – created by Rameses in emulation of a similar dual temple sanctuary built further south by Amenhotep III. The Great Temple at Abu Simbel was dedicated principally to the god Re-Horakhty, and the Small Temple dedicated to the goddess Hathor and his Great Wife Nefertari – for whom, in due course, the king also built a truly magnificent tomb in the Valley of the Queens.

In his attempts to emulate his father in warfare, Rameses II also appears as a man in a hurry. In the fifth year of his reign, he led four divisions of the Egyptian army into Syria in order to retake the city of Qadesh, which had recently seceded to the Hittite Empire.

Thoroughly misled by the Hittite king Muwatallis, the Egyptian army was nearly routed within sight of the walls of Qadesh – Rameses only escaping with his life through his own tenacity and the support of Egyptian reinforcements from the coast – which ultimately resulted in a stalemate (although Qadesh remained in Hittite hands).

On highly dubious grounds, and ignoring the occasional complaints of misrepresentation from the Hittite court, Rameses II presented the Battle of Qadesh as a great personal victory. A vivid account appears on many of the buildings constructed during his reign – an early example of 'fake news' – carved on the first pylon at Luxor temple and the north wall of the Great Temple at Abu Simbel, for example. Despite the level of irritation these claims caused the Hittite king, a peace treaty was eventually signed between the Egyptian and Hittite empires in 1259 BC.

Rameses II – this 'young man in a hurry' – could not know in advance that he would occupy the throne for 67 years. He was buried in the Valley of the Kings, in what must have been a most magnificent tomb that was sadly destroyed in antiquity by flooding. His ruined memorial temple (including a palace), known as the Ramesseum, still stands on the west

OPPOSITE:

Hathor Chapel, Memorial Temple of Thutmose III, Deir el-Bahari
The ruins of the memorial temple of Thutmose III lie between those of Montjuhotep II and Hatshepsut at Deir el-Bahari. A small chapel was created here in honour of the goddess Hathor (now in the Egyptian Museum, Cairo). Here Thutmose (left) makes an offering to Amun-Re, who is seated on a throne.

bank at Luxor and remains impressive to this day.

Indeed, perhaps Rameses II lived too long, for he was succeeded by an already elderly son, Merenptah, who may have been less able than some of his long-dead brothers to provide the leadership and security that Egypt was to need, although he had probably already shouldered considerable responsibility in his father's declining years.

External pressure was quickly exerted on the kingdom by 'Libyan' tribes to the west, and the arrival of an enigmatic group of raiders known as the 'Sea Peoples' along the Mediterranean coast. Both appearances at the borders were harbingers of greater problems to come.

THE NEW KINGDOM DECLINES

Merenptah's reign lasted 10 years, after which he was succeeded by his son, Seti II (1200–1194 BC) – already in his middle years – whose throne appears to have been promptly usurped, in part, by his son Amenmeses, who temporarily ruled parts of Nubia and the area immediately around Thebes. By the time Seti II regained control of Egypt, he had only a year to live. He was succeeded by the young king Siptah (1194–1188 BC), under the regency of his mother Tawoseret (1188–1186 BC), who, after the death of Siptah, ruled Egypt as a female king. However, two years later she in turn was overthrown, bringing the Nineteenth Dynasty to a close.

The story of the 20th Dynasty (1186–1069 BC) is one of restoration following the disorder at the end of the Nineteenth Dynasty, but more significantly, the constant need to defend the borders of Egypt. Rameses III (1184–1153 BC), whose magnificent memorial temple stands at Medinet Habu (on the West Bank opposite Luxor), successfully, but temporarily, stemmed the tide of renewed Libyan military incursions – although many Libyans also entered Egypt peacefully and settled in the Delta during his reign.

More seriously, the Sea Peoples – probably originating from southern Italy and the Aegean – rampaged through Asia Minor and Syria and posed a substantial threat to Egypt. In a major campaign recorded on the walls of Medinet Habu, Rameses III successfully defeated the Sea Peoples both by land and sea, but perhaps inevitably these wars took their toll on the economic and political life of Egypt, for which Rameses III appears to have been blamed, and he was assassinated.

Rameses III was the last great king to bear that name, although another eight were to follow. After his reign, the New Kingdom slowly drifted into lifelessness, and Egypt was never to have the position on the world stage that it had previously carved out for itself. Again, the state itself was to be fractured between north and south. In addition, the technology of warfare within the region was to shift from copper to iron – of which Egypt had little – leaving it to eventually languish at the mercy of emerging powers to the east and, later, to the north.

OPPOSITE:

Deir el-Bahari, West Bank, Luxor
This World Heritage Site contains a complex of memorial temples and tombs. The memorial temple of Montjuhotep II (2055–2004 BC) lies in the centre distance, and the temple of Hatshepsut lies in the foreground. The memorial temple of Thutmose III lies between them, but was severely damaged in antiquity by a landslide. Included in other burials found here were the mummies of Seti I and Rameses II, among other kings – hidden in a cache to keep them safe from tomb robbers – and a large number of priests from Karnak.

Djehuty and His Mother Receive Offerings, Tomb of Djehuty, Sheikh Abd el-Qurna

Djehuty was a scribe and steward to the high priest, and 'head of all the weavers of Amun' in the temple of Amun at Karnak during the reign of Amenhotep II (1427–1400 BC). Here, he is seen with his mother receiving offerings intended to sustain the dead. 'Djehuty' is the Egyptian name of the god Thoth.

ABOVE:
Tomb of Thutmose III, Valley of the Kings
Excavated far from the entrance to the valley, the tomb of Thutmose III was one of the first to be cut. The yellow background is unusual and is painted with an early version of the *Amduat* ('That Which is in the Afterworld'), in which the dead king takes the same journey as the sun god Re, from the setting of the sun to its rising, when he joins with Re for eternity. The beautiful cartouche-shaped quartzite sarcophagus (painted red) of the king remains in the tomb.

OPPOSITE:
Head of Amenhotep III, Temple of Mut, Karnak
Thought to be of Amenhotep III, this red granite head is now in the British Museum. Here the king wears the double crown of Upper and Lower Egypt. A testament to ancient Egyptian engineering, when it was discovered in 1817, it took eight days to move this four-ton, 3m (10ft) high piece 2.5km (1.5 miles) to Luxor.

BELOW:
'Kateriskos' Vase, Palace of Amenhotep III, Malqata
The techniques associated with true glass production probably entered Egypt from southwest Asia around 1500 BC. By the reign of Amenhotep III (1390–1352 BC), Egypt was producing sophisticated pieces like this vessel found at the king's palace in Malqata on the West Bank at Thebes (now in the Walters Art Museum, Baltimore). The glass was not blown, but formed around a clay core.

ABOVE:
Solar Court, Luxor Temple
The spacious Solar Court of Amenhotep III (52 x 46m/ 170 x 151ft) is approached by a colonnade of 14 open-papyrus capital columns. A masterpiece of ancient Egyptian architecture, the graceful papyrus-bud capital columns stand in two rows on three sides of the court.

LEFT:
Amenhotep, Son of Hapu, Great Temple of Amun, Karnak
Commoner, scribe and architect, Amenhotep rose in the favour of Amenhotep III to the level that he was allowed a temple at Medinet Habu. Here, he is shown as a young man at work as a scribe. The hieroglyphic text on the scroll in his lap records that he oversaw the work that produced the so-called 'Colossi of Memnon' at Amenhotep III's memorial temple.

OPPOSITE:
Funerary Mask of Tuya, Tomb of Yuya and Tuya, Valley of the Kings
Yuya and Tuya were the parents of Tiy, the Great Wife of Amenohotep III. They were held in sufficient regard that they were allowed a tomb in the Valley, though of more modest proportions than the royal tombs. Although the tomb had been robbed of its smaller objects, much still remained when it was opened in 1905. Yuya looks out here from his gold-leaf covered, mummy-shaped sarcophagus, now in the Egyptian Museum, Cairo.

ABOVE:

Four Vases in the Name of Yuya, Tomb of Yuya and Tuya, Valley of the Kings

These unusual vases were made of limestone painted to imitate Egyptian alabaster. The lids are topped with a black and white calf, an ibex, a frog, and a red and white calf. The ibex vessel has a spout also in the form of an ibex. Only the first few centimetres of the interior is carved out, and the inscription reads 'the Osiris Yuya justified' – indicating that the vases were intended for use by the deceased. (Egyptian Museum, Cairo.)

ABOVE:

Chair of Princess Sitamun, Tomb of Yuya and Tuya, Valley of the Kings

Sitamun was the granddaughter of Yuya and Tuya, and, presumably, she had this fine chair placed in her grandparents' tomb. On the back of the chair (in the Egyptian Museum, Cairo), a young girl presents the princess with a large necklace. She already wears a necklace, earrings, a bracelet and a long pleated skirt. In her right hand, she holds a *sistrum* rattle associated with religious rituals.

FOLLOWING PAGES:

'Colossi of Memnon', Memorial Temple of Amenhotep III, Luxor

Described for centuries as statues of the fictional Greek hero Memnon, these 18m-high (59ft) statues of Amenhotep III originally stood in front of the great memorial temple of the king that was destroyed by an earthquake soon after it was completed. Small statues of Amenhotep's Great Wife Tiy, and of his mother Mutemwiya, stand beside the king's legs.

ABOVE:
Colossal Statue of Amenhotep IV, Temple of the Aten, Karnak
Now in the Egyptian Museum in Cairo, this statue was associated with the Temple of Amun at Karnak that was shortly to be suppressed – along with its priesthood – by Akhenaten from his new capital at Akhetaten (Amarna). The extraordinary features of the king's image illustrate the beginning of the 'Amarna Style'.

ABOVE:

House Shrine of Akhenaten, Nefertiti and Daughters, Amarna
This delightful image was probably part of an altar to the divine family, and may be intended to represent how they appeared in life within a particular palace window to the people of Akhetaten. Sunrays ending in *ankh* life signs emanate from the Aten to a scene of the strange, other forms of the king, queen and their three playful, eldest daughters Meretaten, Meketaten and Ankhesenpaaten. (Egyptian Museum, Berlin.)

LEFT:

Bust of Nefertiti, Workshop of the Sculptor Thutmose, Amarna
As iconic as the funerary mask of Tutankhamun, the limestone and stucco bust of Nefertiti was found with similar pieces in the remains of Thutmose's workshop in 1912. She wears an unusual headdress ('cap crown') known from other depictions of her. In more 'classical Egyptian', rather than 'Amarna', style, the bust may have been simply a model that could be followed by the workshop for official statues.

ABOVE:

Fragment of a painted pavement, South Palace, Amarna
Found in 1896, these wonderful representations of wild ducks flying in the marshes were part of the painted plaster floors within a secondary palace at Amarna. This naturalistic image of the ducks is typical of the Amarna style, but such scenes also had a deeper significance in terms of ancient Egyptian creation myths – the first land to emerge from the primeval waters being marshes.

FOLLOWING PAGES:

The Valley of the Kings, West Bank, Luxor
Probably chosen as a burial place because of the pyramidal hill ('al-Qurn') that dominates the area, the Valley of the Kings – in fact, two valleys – was used for a period of about 500 years (around 1504 to 1069 BC) for the rock-cut tombs of pharaohs, members of their family and honoured nobles. Of 63 known tombs, only about 20 were built for kings. The entrance to Tutankhamun's tomb can be seen on the left-hand side of the valley in the foreground (below the square area).

OPPOSITE:

The Throne of Tutankhamun (detail), Valley of the Kings
In one of the most touching scenes to have survived from ancient Egypt, and typical of the Amarna style, Tutankhamun and his wife Ankhesenamun form a scene below the Aten and its life-giving rays. The king sits comfortably with an arm resting on a padded throne, while Ankhesenamun spreads ointment on his shoulder. The wooden throne (in the Grand Egyptian Museum, Cairo) is lined with gold and inlaid with silver, semi-precious stones and glass paste.

ABOVE:

Container and canopic jars, Tomb of Tutankhamun
These canopic jars contained the internal organs (stomach, intestines, lungs and liver) removed from the king's body during the mummification process – each stored in a separate solid gold sarcophagus. Each jar has the image of the king as a lid.

The whole container has an image of the goddesses Isis, Nephthys, Neith and Selket on the corners to protect these preserved parts of Tutankhamun's body. (Grand Egyptian Museum, Cairo.)

OPPOSITE TOP:
Necklace with Nekhbet pendant, Tomb of Tutankhamun
This crooked-wing pendant of the vulture goddess Nehkbet, patron of Upper Egypt and protector of the pharaoh, was found within the mummy wrappings of the king. Nekhbet holds the *shen* sign of eternity in her talons. The piece, in the Grand Egyptian Museum, is remarkable for the modelling of the vulture's head in gold – including the characteristic wrinkles and short feathers of the neck.

OPPOSITE BOTTOM:
Ostrich feather fan, Tomb of Tutankhamun
Decorated with gold leaf on wood, the fan (mounted on a 1m/3ft pole, and in the Grand Egyptian Museum, Cairo) shows the king in a typical hunting scene. Mounted on a lightweight chariot pulled by two decorated horses, Tutankhamun shoots arrows at an ostrich, while a hunting dog gives chase. The original brown and white feathers were the result of a hunt in the desert east of Heliopolis.

ABOVE:
Fowl-Hunting Scene, Tomb of Nebamun, Theban Necropolis
Several scenes from the tomb (about 1350 BC) were hacked from the walls of the temple scribe Nebamun's tomb in 1820. These masterpieces of ancient Egyptian art are now on display in the British Museum. Here, Nebamun captures waterfowl in the marshes, 'enjoying himself and seeing beauty', and forever young in the afterlife – accompanied by his wife Hatshepsut, daughter, and a cat.

PREVIOUS PAGES:

Burial Chamber North Wall, Tomb of Tutankhamun, Valley of the Kings
The burial chamber was almost entirely filled with the shrine that held the body of the king inside a nest of smaller shrines, the sarcophagus and coffins. On the north wall, the sky goddess Nut greets Tutankhamun (left). To the right, the king embraces Osiris accompanied by a principal part of his soul (with the *ka* symbol above his head).

RIGHT:

Antechamber, Tomb of Horemheb, Valley of the Kings
The accession of Horemheb (1323–1295 BC) marked the end of the Amarna Period and laid the foundations for the Nineteenth Dynasty. The blue-grey background of the tomb accentuates the exquisite paintings within the well chamber, antechamber and burial chamber within his tomb. Here, on the northeast wall of the antechamber, the king is greeted by the goddess Hathor (left) and makes an offering to the god Horus.

South Wall, Tomb of Ramose, Sheikh Abd el-Qurna

One of the most fascinating and beautiful tombs in the Theban Necropolis belonged to the hereditary nobleman and vizier Ramose, and combines Amarna and traditional styles (early in the reign of Amenhotep IV/Akhenaten). The south wall is covered by a funerary procession, including the grave goods being carried to the tomb, the coffin on a boat being dragged on a sled and a group of mourning women and children.

123

OPPOSITE:

Sennefer and his wife Hatshepsut, Tomb of Sennefer, Sheikh Abd el-Qurna

Dating to the reign of Amenhotep II (1427–1400 BC), the sculptor of this piece, now in the Louvre, clearly attempted to create a portrait of the king's head clerk and his wife. Hatshepsut wears a substantial wig ending in braids. She has full cheeks and tapered black eye make-up. Sennefer, by contrast, has a thinner face with prominent cheekbones.

ABOVE:

Field Inspectors, Tomb Chapel of Menna, Sheikh Abd el-Qurna

Also to be found in the 'Valley of the Nobles', and probably dating to the reign of Amenhotep III (1390–1352 BC), the beautiful tomb of Menna, 'overseer of the fields of Amun', includes scenes of the everyday life of ancient Egyptians. Here the workers harvest, thresh and winnow the grain.

OPPOSITE TOP:

Ladies and a Harpist at a Banquet, Tomb of Nakht, Sheikh Abd el-Qurna

Nakht was an 'astronomer of Amun' during the reign of Thutmose IV (1400–1390 BC). In this continuous scene, elegant ladies sit on the ground: one passes fruit to another; to the right of them, a lady smells a lotus flower while listening to a harpist, who is concentrating on the music. The ladies have cones of perfumed fat on their heads that would melt as time passed.

OPPOSITE BOTTOM:

Dead in the Field of Reeds, Tomb of Sennedjem, Deir el-Medina

The tomb of the senior artisan Sennedjem lies above the walled village of the artisans at Deir el-Medina, and included the furniture from his home. Those same artists who decorated the royal and noble tombs in the Valley of the Kings decorated these smaller tombs, producing masterpieces on a human scale. Here, Sennedjem and his wife Iyneferti are seen harvesting in the fields in the afterlife.

ABOVE:

Ceiling with Bull's Head, Tomb of Inherkau, Deir el-Medina

Inherkau was the 'Foreman of the Lord of Two Lands in the Place of Truth', overseeing the artisans working in the Valley of the Kings during the reign of Rameses III (1184–1153 BC). On the ceiling of this small tomb are traditional Egyptian geometric patterns perhaps imitating reed matting (left), and spiral designs surrounding bulls' heads (right) borrowed from far-off Minoan Crete.

128

Seti I and Prince Rameses before the King List, Abydos Temple
In this famous scene from the temple built by Seti I (1294–1279 BC) at the ancient royal site at Abydos, the king stands with his son, the future Rameses II, before the list of 76 'legitimate' kings of Egypt (it excludes the Hyksos kings, Hatshepsut and the Amarna kings). Both the unusual presence here of the crown prince (wearing the side lock of youth), and the list itself, were intended to establish beyond doubt the legitimacy of the newly established Nineteenth dynasty and the planned succession.

ABOVE:
Bound Syrian Prisoners, Great Temple, Abu Simbel
The internal strife associated with the rule of Akhenaten saw a reduction of Egyptian influence in the Levant, resurgence in Nubia, and an increase in pressure from 'Libya' to the west. Much of the reigns of Horemheb, Rameses I and Seti I were occupied with combatting or thwarting the ambitions of the Hittite empire spreading southward from its homeland in Anatolia.

RIGHT:

Great Hypostyle Hall, Karnak Temple
One of the masterpieces of ancient Egyptian architecture, the great pillared hall at Karnak is a testament to Seti I's interest in the arts in addition to war. The whole hall – standing before the innermost shine complex of Amun-Re – represented the primeval swamp land that emerged at the creation.

ABOVE:
The Great Hypostyle Hall (detail), Karnak Temple
The 134 columns laid out in 16 rows originally supported a roof, and the hall was dimly lit through stone slat windows at the top. The decoration of the hall was completed by Rameses II (1279–1213 BC), who had his own name carved on every surface, sometimes obliterating that of his father, Seti I.

RIGHT:
South Wall of the Burial Chamber, The Tomb of Seti I, Valley of the Kings
Perhaps the greatest artistic achievement of Seti I's reign, his tomb in the Valley of the Kings heightened interest in ancient Egypt in the early Nineteenth century – large crowds gathered in 1821 in both London and Paris to see exhibitions of paintings from the tomb. Here, the goddess Nephthys spreads her wings protectively just below the magnificent vaulted ceiling – the first occurrence of an astronomical depiction of the northern night sky to appear in a burial chamber.

LEFT:

Rear Side Chamber, The Tomb of Seti I, Valley of the Kings
Although much of its great beauty still remains, Seti I's tomb was heavily damaged by flooding soon after its discovery, and by the unsubtle removal of many reliefs by collectors. The tomb was, however, decorated throughout. Here in a side chamber, an enthroned figure of Osiris (right) graces one of the pillars, while scenes from the *Amduat* appear on the walls.

ABOVE:

Wooden Coffin of Seti I, Deir el-Bahari Cache
Neither Seti I nor his son Rameses II were destined to remain for eternity in the tombs that were created for them. Robbery of the royal tombs led to extensive damage to the mummy of Seti I, which led to the body being removed from the tomb during the Twenty-First Dynasty (under Siamun 978–959 BC), and moved again during the reign of Shoshenq I (945–924 BC) to a cache of royal and noble mummies at Deir el-Bahari. One of the original wooden coffins of the king (originally gilded) travelled with Seti I and can be seen in the Egyptian Museum in Cairo.

OPPOSITE:

Rameses II in the Blue *Khepresh* Crown, Thebes
Perhaps the greatest image to have survived of the king, this black diorite statue of Rameses II as a young king wearing the blue crown of Egypt (or *Khepresh*) and holding the *heqa* sceptre is now in the Egyptian Museum in Turin. The king wears a long robe, rather than the kilt that would have been worn in battle. Beside his right leg is a small statue of Rameses' Great Wife Nefertari.

ABOVE:

The Ramesseum from the air, West Bank, Luxor
The memorial temple of Rameses II comprised two gateways (left), the main temple complex (centre), including a 48-column hypostyle hall, and a large number of vaulted storage rooms (right). Within the confines of the temple there was a small palace used by Rameses II during his lifetime, particularly during the 'Beautiful Festival of the Valley', when the image of Amun-Re made its procession among the temples of the West Bank.

LEFT:

Colossal Statue of Rameses II, The Ramesseum

The collapsed seated statue of the king, thought to be – at around 17.5m/57ft high, and weighing more than 1000 tons – the largest colossus created in Egypt, stood in the first court by the second gateway (or pylon). The statue probably collapsed during the Roman Period, and, in its ruined state, inspired – at a distance – Percy Bysshe Shelley's 1818 poem 'Ozymandias'.

ABOVE:

Bust of Meritamun, Temple of Meritamun, The Ramesseum

Meritamun was a daughter of Rameses II and Nefertari, and became a Great Wife of the king at some time after her mother's death. This statue, now in the Egyptian Museum, is probably, though not certainly, of Meritamun. Two cobras wear the white and red crowns of Egypt at her brow, and her crown (or *modius*) is composed of the *uraeus* cobras and sun disks.

PREVIOUS PAGES:

Inner Ramp and Staircase, Tomb of Nefertari, Valley of the Queens
The brilliant colours against a white background of Nefertari's tomb produce an effect of unequalled beauty. Here, Nefertari makes an offering beside an overflowing table to the goddess Isis (and Nephthys to the right).

BELOW:

Goddess Maat, Burial Chamber (niche), Tomb of Nefertari
Within a niche in the burial chamber, a monochrome image of the goddess Maat appears. Maat personified the central concepts of justice, truth and order that ruled the lives of all ancient Egyptians. It was against the feather of Maat that the heart of the deceased was weighed after death.

OPPOSITE:

Nefertari led by the hand by Isis (watercolour), Burial Chamber, Tomb of Nefertari
Painted by Charles K. Wilkinson in 1922–23, this watercolour (from the collection of the Metropolitan Museum of Art, New York), is an example of the care taken to accurately record the detail of tombs like that of Nefertari. Here, the goddess Isis (right) leads Nefertari towards the afterlife.

OPPOSITE:
First Pylon, Luxor Temple
Early in his reign, Rameses II added a new court and pylon (through which the temple is entered today) to the temple that had been built by Amenhotep III (1390–1352 BC). The pylon was constructed soon after the battle of Qadesh, which is portrayed on the outside walls. One seated statue and two striding statues of the king originally flanked the gate to either side. There were two obelisks in front of the pylon – one now stands in the Place de la Concorde in Paris.

ABOVE:
Weighing of the Heart, Papyrus of Ani, Tomb of Ani, Thebes
Now in the British Museum, the papyrus of Ani (about 1250 BC) shows the gods (top) passing judgment on the scribe (left). The god Anubis steadies the scale upon which the heart of the deceased is weighed against the feather of Maat. To the top left of the scale, the human-headed *ba* bird – representing the unique personality of the deceased's soul – perches ready to take flight to the afterlife should the judgment be in Ani's favour.

PREVIOUS PAGES:
The Great Temple, Abu Simbel
The two rock-cut temples of Abu Simbel lie near the border between Egypt and Sudan. The exterior of the Great Temple, principally composed of four colossal statues of Rameses II, imitates a pylon of a free-standing temple. The temple was dedicated to the god Re-Horakhty, the noontime form of the sun god Re. The sanctuary contains statues of the gods Ptah, Amun-Re, Rameses II as a god and Re-Horakhty.

BELOW:
Interior of the Small Temple, Abu Simbel
The Small Temple is generally characterized by a more delicate touch suitable to its dedication to the goddess of femininity, Hathor. Nefertari, for whom Rameses built the temple, appears frequently here in the company of gods and goddesses. The pillars of the first hall are crowned by an image of Hathor.

OPPOSITE TOP:
Small Temple, Abu Simbel
The exterior of the Small Temple is composed of four statues of Rameses II and two of Nefertari. Unusually in an ancient Egyptian context, the statues of Nefertari are almost the same height as those of the king – indicative of the status of the Great Wife as a favourite, not least as the mother of the first crown prince Amunherkhepeshef.

OPPOSITE BOTTOM:
Interior of the Great Temple, Abu Simbel
The hypostyle hall of the Great Temple contains eight colossal statues of the king in the form of the god Osiris. The entire north wall recounts the battle of Qadesh in almost comic-strip fashion. Beyond the hypostyle hall is a further hall in which Rameses greets many gods and goddesses – including himself in divine form.

ABOVE:
Raised Relief, Tomb of Ramose, Sheikh Abd el-Qurna
In the early years of Rameses II's reign, the fine technique of raised relief – spectacularly illustrated here from the earlier Amarna Period tomb of the vizier Ramose – gave way to the quicker and cheaper technique of sunk relief, where the subject was carved, often deeply, into the rock surface. Given the extensive building program instituted by the king throughout Egypt, there were probably too few skilled craftsmen available, and much reliance was placed on the labour of prisoners of war.

OPPOSITE:
Shabti of Merenptah, Thebes
When Rameses II died at the age of about 90, he was succeeded by his 14th son, Merenptah (1213–1203 BC), who was already late into his middle age. Egypt was soon after thrown into crisis by attacks from Libyan tribesmen and the enigmatic 'Sea Peoples' along the Mediterranean coast. Although these attacks were repulsed by Merenptah, they were harbingers of more difficult times to come. This small statue (or *shabti*) of the king in the form of the god Osiris can be seen in the Metropolitan Museum in New York.

LEFT:

Merenptah Stele, Temple of Merenptah, Thebes
The stele – in the Egyptian Museum, Cairo – mostly records the victories of the king over the Libyan tribesmen who were increasingly problematic. It is notable also for its description of campaigns in Canaan. On the 27th line of the hieroglyphic inscription is a set of signs that most scholars interpret as referring to Israel – the earliest reference from ancient Egypt.

ABOVE:

First Pylon, Medinet Habu, West Bank, Luxor

Less visited than it deserves, the memorial temple of Rameses III (1184–1153 BC) can be seen as a better-preserved copy of the Ramesseum of Rameses II. On the faces of the first pylon, Rameses III is seen in the traditional smiting scenes before Amun-Re (left) and Re-Horakhty (right). An unusual stele inside the doorway records a speech by the king urging the Egyptians to stand by him – an indication of the troubled times as Libyans and Sea Peoples attacked.

OPPOSITE:
Bull hunting scene, First Pylon, Medinet Habu
Rameses III drives his chariot deep into the marshy banks of the Nile to hunt wild bulls in this scene to the rear of the south tower of the first pylon. Fish and birds flee in panic at the king's approach. Such a scene – beautifully portrayed here – would be interpreted as not only demonstrating the king's prowess, but also his ability to keep the powers of chaos at bay from the land.

RIGHT:
Prisoner Tiles, Gateway of the Palace of Rameses III, Medinet Habu
These faience tiles of an Amorite (left) and a Philistine (right) once stood on the right side of the entrance gate to Rameses III's palace at Medinet Habu, together with similar tiles of defeated peoples – including Syrians, Nubians and Libyans. Rameses III was the last great pharaoh to bear that name, and the New Kingdom began its slow decline after his reign. (Museum of Fine Arts, Boston.)

155

OPPOSITE:
Rameses VI with a Prisoner, Temple of Amun-Re, Karnak
Rameses VI (reigned 1143–1136 BC) is seen here in a pose that was symptomatic of the times – an axe in one hand and holding a Libyan prisoner by the hair in the other. A lion peers out at his feet. Typical of such pieces found at Karnak, an inscription to the side declares the king's devotion to Amun-Re. (Luxor Museum.)

ABOVE:
Rameses IX casket, Cache, Deir el-Bahari
This pretty wood and ivory casket dating to the reign of Rameses IX (1126–1108 BC) was found among a cache of royal and noble mummies at Deir el-Bahari, and is now in the Egyptian Museum, Cairo. An inscription giving the full royal titles of the king runs around the box, which was closed by running a string around two knobs (the top knob is missing).

The Late Period

Shortly after the death of Rameses XI (1099–1069 BC), the last king of the Twentieth Dynasty, Egypt divided into two realms, marking the beginning of the Third Intermediate Period (1069–747 BC). The kings of Thebes (derived from the ranks of the high priests of Amun) ruled the area from Aswan northward to the border of the Fayoum; and the kings to the north (beginning with Nesibanebdjedet I [Smendes], 1069–1043 BC, the first king of the Twenty-First Dynasty) ruled the remainder of the country from Tanis in the delta southward.

During this period, both kingdoms showed no hesitation in emptying the tombs of their royal predecessors of their riches. As a result, the tombs at Tanis – which were found intact in 1939 – acted as a storeroom of ancient Egyptian treasures rivalling those of Tutankhamun.

LIBYAN KINGS

The Tanis tombs not only included kings, but also senior military men, many of whose families were from Libya. In due course, it was a Libyan, Osorkon the Elder (984–978 BC), who became king – presaging a line of Libyan kings of the Twenty-Second Dynasty (945–715 BC) and Twenty-Third Dynasty (818–793 BC), beginning with Shoshenq I (945–924 BC). Shoshenq founded yet another new capital city at Bubastis in the Delta, and restored the authority of the monarchy over the south by installing his own son as High Priest of Amun.

After establishing effective control over all Egypt, Shoshenq I lead the Egyptian army in attacking Israel and Judah (925 BC). However, he was to die just a short time after this first expedition to the northeast of the Egyptian border in 200 years.

OPPOSITE:
Pectoral of Shoshenq II, Tomb of Psusennes II, Tanis
The grave of the Libyan king Shoshenq II (reigned about 890 BC) was found in 1839 within the tomb of Psusennes II (959–945 BC). The only ruler of the Twenty-Second Dynasty whose resting place remained intact, he may have been the son of Shoshenq I (945–924 BC), the founder of the dynasty. The pectoral has a lapis lazuli solar scarab pushing the sun disk across the sky at its centre. The two *uraeus* cobras wear only the white crown of Upper Egypt.

For the most part, the Libyan kings who followed Shoshenq concentrated their efforts on maintaining power within Egypt – although by 818 BC, the kingdom was rapidly fragmenting into city-states (a period referred to as the Twenty-Third Dynasty), and all the while a new force was emerging on Egypt's southern border.

THE KUSHITE KINGS

The kings of Kush (part of modern Sudan) had, over centuries, been increasing their power from their capital, Napata, and they were kings with a mission. The Kushites believed themselves to be the true heirs of ancient Egypt, and particularly of the cult of the god Amun – who was said to have emerged from the mountain of Gebel Barkal within their lands.

The Kushite army had pushed to the border with Egypt before, but it was King Piye (747–716 BC) who carried out what might be considered a holy war, and took Thebes (including the temple of Amun at Karnak, where he was crowned).

In response, the Libyan kings to the north formed a coalition and marched south, but were ferociously pushed back by Piye, who took Memphis by storm and made the northern kings his vassals – thus inaugurating the Twenty-Fifth Dynasty (747–332 BC – the city-state of Saite resisted briefly with one king, Bakenrenef, of the Twenty-Fourth Dynasty).

OPPOSITE:
City of Tanis, Nile Delta
Although restoration work is continuing there, the City of Tanis, in the northeast Nile Delta, is best known for its scattered fields of ruins and fallen obelisks. Many of these were brought from Rameses II's royal residence of Pirameses when that city was abandoned. A great temple of Amun-Re was built here during the Twenty-First and Twenty-Second Dynasties (1069–715 BC) together with temples dedicated to Mut and Khonsu – mirroring those at Karnak far to the south.

It appears that Shabaqa (716–702 BC), Piye's brother, was the king who subdued the last resistance in 715 BC, becoming ruler of a united land that stretched from modern Khartoum to the Nile Delta.

Perhaps the greatest of the Kushite kings was a son of Piye, Taharqa (690–664 BC), who was crowned, as was the Egyptian tradition, at Memphis in 690 BC. He added a new set of columns to the first court of Karnak temple, and further south in the Kushite homelands he constructed a new royal cemetery at Nuri, close to Napata, where his own 50m-high (164-ft) pyramid was built. Across the Nile, he added to the temple of Amun at Gebel Barkal, constructing a new chapel within the mountain and gilding the rock pinnacle there, so that it might catch the morning sun.

ASSYRIA ATTACKS

Taharqa did not ignore the defence of Egypt, however – even allying with the king of Judah, Hezekiah, as he attempted to thwart the western expansion of the Assyrian Empire. Yet the days of the Kushite kingdom were nonetheless numbered.

In 674 BC, Esarhaddon, the Assyrian king, invaded Egypt but was initially repulsed by Taharqa. In 671 BC, Esarhaddon returned, took Memphis, and forced Taharqa to retreat south. The Assyrian conqueror promoted local rulers as his vassals, before leaving again for the Assyrian homelands in modern Iraq.

Soon afterward, Taharqa reasserted control in the north, but was defeated by the new king of Assyria, Ashurbanipal, and, this time, he was pushed back to Nubia.

Of the Libyan rulers in the north, only Nekau I (Necho) of Sais (672–664 BC) was ultimately considered to be loyal to Assyria –

although he lost his life to Taharqa's nephew and successor, Tanutamun (664–656 BC), in a brief period of Kushite resurgence.

In 663 BC, Assyria invaded with full force, moving so far south that they sacked the great temple at Karnak. Forced by a rebellion at home to withdraw, the Assyrian king installed Nekau's son Psamtek I (664–610 BC) as king, inaugurating the Twenty-Sixth Dynasty.

Their attention distracted by a resurgent Babylon to their south, it seems that the Assyrians did not initially notice that Psamtek had different ideas about his vassal status. Within 10 years he had reunited north and south with the help of his young daughter Neiriqert (Nitokris) who was, in time, installed as senior priestess in Karnak (she was to live on into her 80s).

Psamtek increased the defensive capabilities of Egypt by the installation of Greek and other mercenaries on the northeast border. These soldiers were used to great effect to keep the Babylonians – the new threat from the east – at bay under Psamtek's son Nekau II (610–595 BC).

THE PERSIAN INVASION

Combining his own interests with those of Assyria, Nekau II pushed west through the Levant to the Euphrates River, but was quickly pushed back by Babylon.

The later years of the 'Saite Period' were similarly occupied by military campaigns in the Levant and Libya, but also by civil war between kings Wahire and Ahmose II, which Ahmose (570–526 BC) eventually won.

While Ahmose was on his deathbed, a new power to the east in the shape of the Persians (having disposed of the Babylonians) appeared on the frontier. His unfortunate successor, Psamtek III (526–525 BC) was swept aside and surrendered to the Persians at Memphis.

The Persian king Kambyses and his successors took control of Egypt directly (the Twenty-Seventh Dynasty, 525–404 BC). However, a resurgence of local authority occurred under Amyrtaios of Sais (404–339 BC – the Twenty-Eighth Dynasty), and after his execution, under King Naeferud I and his family from Mendes (399–380 BC – the Twenty-Ninth Dynasty); then, following revolts, the family of general Nakhtnebef (as Nectanebo I) from Sebennytos (380–343 BC – the Thirtieth Dynasty). The last native king of Egypt, Nakhthorheb (Nectanebo II – 360–343 BC), fought bravely, but was ultimately forced to retreat south as the Persian king Artaxerxes III forced his way into Egypt. He may have found safety in Kush – or, as legend would have it, in the court of Philip II of Macedon.

Egypt was not to be an independent state again for 1500 years.

The Persian kings ruled Egypt directly again for a short period (343–332 BC); it is said their rule was so burdensome that when a new army appeared on the borders of Egypt, the people welcomed them with open arms.

OPPOSITE:

Head of Taharqa, Temple of Amun-Re, Karnak
Now in the Nubian Museum, Aswan, this colossal black granite head of the great Nubian king Taharqa (690–664 BC) was probably associated with the buildings he created at the temple of Amun-Re at Karnak. He wears a Nubian cap crown and a low circular *modius* (crown). The whole headdress would have been covered in sheet gold.

OPPOSITE:
Triad of Osiris belonging to Osorkon II, Tanis
This magnificent solid gold and lapis lazuli pendant of Osiris (centre), Isis (right), and Horus is now in the Louvre Museum, Paris; it probably belonged to, and protected, the Libyan king Osorkon II (872–831 BC) during his lifetime. The figure of a crouching Osiris is unusual in ancient Egyptian art. Osorkon appointed his son Nimlot to the High Priesthood of Thebes, ensuring the loyalty of Upper Egypt.

RIGHT:
Head of Shabataka, Temple of Amun-Re, Karnak
Shabataka (713–705 BC) was probably the son of the Kushite king Piye (745–713 BC), the founder of the Twenty-Fifth Dynasty. His successor, Shabaka (705–690 BC), reduced the last resistance in Egypt to rule a kingdom stretching over an area from near modern Khartoum to the Nile Delta. (Nubian Museum, Aswan.)

LEFT:
Statue of Nefertem, Serapeum, Saqqara
Portraying the son of the god Ptah and the lioness goddess Sekhmet, this piece is dated to the Saite Period (672–525 BC) and is in the Egyptian Museum, Cairo. Nefertem is identified by the open lotus flower (the leaves of which were originally picked out in blue enamel) and two plumes. The lotus plant was the first to open according to one version of the ancient Egyptian story of creation.

OPPOSITE:
Sarcophagus of Psusennes I, Tomb of Psusennes I, Tanis
The intact tomb of Pasebkhanut (Psusennes I – 1039–991 BC, Twenty-First Dynasty, Third Intermediate Period) was found at Tanis in 1940 and is the only ancient Egyptian tomb that was not robbed (Tutankhamun's tomb was entered twice by thieves). While wooden objects did not survive, the tomb is remarkable for its many gold and silver objects. Here, the face of the king has been created from silver and gold on the innermost of the three sarcophagi. (Egyptian Museum, Cairo.)

OPPOSITE:
Funerary Mask of Psusennes I, Tomb of Psusennes I, Tanis
This masterpiece among the treasures from Tanis in the Egyptian Museum, Cairo, is made from sheet gold ('the flesh of the gods'), lapis lazuli and glass paste. The false beard curves upwards slightly to indicate the divine status of the dead king – a glass-paste-filled groove runs along the side of the face, imitating the string with which the beard was tied on.

ABOVE:
Mummy Plaque, Tomb of Psusennes I, Tanis
This mummy plaque covered the incision made for the removal of the internal organs during the mummification process, and was intended to protect the mummy from evil forces. The plaque has the protective *wadjet* eye at its centre. The four sons of Horus – Imset, Hapi, Duamutuef and Qebehsenuef – provide additional protection.

OPPOSITE:
Pectoral of Psusennes I, Tomb of Psusennes I, Tanis
The pectoral is made from gold, red and green jasper, blue glass and green feldspar. The winged scarab has the cloisonné cartouche of the king above it, in place of the more usual sun disk. The chain of the necklace – made from gold and coloured stones – ends in a lotus flower. (Egyptian Museum, Cairo.)

RIGHT:
Statue of Isis, Tomb of Psamtek, Saqqara
This fine statue of Isis was found alongside others – of Hathor and Psamtek, and of Osiris – that were clearly made by the same gifted artist for the tomb of the chief scribe and governor of the palace. The slightly smiling goddess sits upon the throne of the king, which she personifies. Over time, Isis assimilated characteristics of other goddesses; here she is seen with the cow's horns of the goddess Hathor. (Egyptian Museum, Cairo.)

LEFT:
Statue of Osiris, Tomb of Psamtek, Saqqara
As is characteristic of depictions of Osiris, here he sits on a throne clothed in a tight-fitting sheath from which only his hands emerge. He holds the *heqa* sceptre and the *neheh* flail of kingship, and wears the *atef* crown, composed of the crown of Upper Egypt with two plumes. (Egyptian Museum, Cairo.)

OPPOSITE:
Head of King Ahmose II, Sais
This finely polished greywacke head is possibly of Ahmose II (570–526 BC) and is now in the Neues Museum, Berlin. It may, in fact, date from the earlier reign of Nekau II (610–595 BC).

Mammisi Birth House, Temple of Dendera

Although dominated today by the Ptolemaic temple, the religious history of Dendera stretched back to the beginning of Egyptian history. Pepi I (2321–2287 BC) appears to have built on the site, and there was probably a temple here during the Eighteenth Dynasty. Nectanebo I (380–362 BC, Thirtieth Dynasty) built a *mammisi* (or divine birth house of the son or daughter of a god and a goddess) here. By association, such a building served to confirm the king's own divine status.

Avenue of the Sphinxes, Luxor
The famous 'Avenue of the Sphinxes' that links the temples of Karnak and Luxor contains hundreds of statues of Nectanebo I with the body of a lion. The king was a great builder, beginning the temple to Isis at Philae, and erecting the first pylon at the Temple of Amun-Re at Karnak, among other construction works.

The Greco-Roman Period

The Persians, under Darius III, were rapidly defeated by the 24-year-old Macedonian king Alexander at the battle of Issus (333 BC), and shortly afterwards he entered Egypt unopposed. He was recognized as the legitimate ruler of Egypt at Memphis, where he was crowned in November 332 BC. Everything in Egypt appeared to make an impression on the young conqueror, and he was wise enough to understand that the key to ruling Egypt was to keep on the right side of its priests.

After touring much of the northern part of Egypt, Alexander headed to the coast – anxious to establish a naval base in order to maintain Macedonian dominance over the eastern Mediterranean. To the west of the Nile Delta he personally marked out what was to become one of the most famous cities and ports of the ancient world, Alexandria.

Alexander left Egypt in 331 BC, never to return. He fought and defeated Darius III again at Gaugamela, this time conclusively, and became the Great King of the Persian Empire. He then fought his way further east to India before returning to Babylon, where he died on 10 June 323 BC aged 32, but not before leaving his new empire 'to the strongest'.

The immediate complexities associated with the succession were resolved by dividing the empire among Alexander's generals – Egypt, Libya and nearby lands were given to the Macedonian general Ptolemy to govern.

In order to more firmly stake his claim as a legitimate (if not <u>the</u> legitimate) heir of Alexander, Ptolemy seized the body of Alexander at Damascus as it was en route from Babylon to Macedonia, and buried the great king in Egypt.

As ruler of a rich country, as an experienced military man and a clever politician – and with the support of the priests of Egypt – Ptolemy

OPPOSITE:
Portrait of Alexander the Great, Alexandria
This marble portrait of Alexander (reigned 332–323 BC) was found in the capital city of Egypt that he founded in 331 BC – Alexandria – and is now in the British Museum. Statues, such as this, were made long after his death and emphasise his youthful, godlike character. Unusually, at the time, Alexander chose to be shown beardless – a style that was to last 500 years among Greek kings and Roman emperors.

was able to successfully thwart the ambitions of his Macedonian rivals, but it was only in 305 BC that he allowed himself to be crowned king of Egypt as Ptolemy I (305–282 BC). Thus began nearly 300 years of Greek rule of Egypt (the Ptolemaic Period, 305–30 BC).

EGYPT UNDER THE PTOLEMIES

Greek became the language of state administration, and Greek gods were fused with many of their Egyptian counterparts (who were increasingly known, like 'Osiris' and 'Isis', by their Greek names). The Ptolemaic kings and queens, though, became virtually indistinguishable from the godlike figures of their Egyptian predecessors, and can be seen as such on the walls of the temples they built.

The complexities associated with these Greek rulers are too great to unravel here, but include overlapping reigns; independent queens whose power was at least equal to that of their male counterparts; murder; sibling marriages; entanglement in the Greek world – both in politics and customs; engagement, latterly, in the ultimately fatal politics of Rome; and rulers who were deposed and later became rulers again.

It was Ptolemy I who began the great library at Alexandria that became, under his successors, a beacon of learning (together with the Temple of the Muses or 'Museum'), which attracted the great minds of antiquity. He also began construction of the more literally vital beacon along this largely featureless coast – the Pharos lighthouse – that, alongside the Great Pyramid, was to feature as one of the seven 'wonders' of the ancient world.

His successors also built on a massive scale from Alexandria to the very southern borders of Egypt. Ptolemy II (285–246 BC) and Queen Arsinoë II (275–268 BC) began work on a new Isis temple at Philae; and Ptolemy III (246–222 BC) and Queen Berenike II (246–221 BC) began construction of a new Horus temple at Edfu; Ptolemy VI (180–145 BC) and Queen Kleopatra II (176–116 BC – Kleopatra or 'Cleopatra' being a popular and well-established Macedonian name) created a new temple at Kom Ombo – all largely regarded today, somewhat mistakenly, as archetypes of ancient Egyptian temple architecture.

During succeeding reigns, the Ptolemies were increasingly drawn into the orbit of the expanding new power of Rome, both as an economic and political partner – so much so that by the reign of Ptolemy VIII (145–116 BC) and Kleopatra II (176–116 BC), Egypt was essentially a protectorate of Rome.

Unsurprisingly, Rome used its influence to gradually weaken the power of Egypt, not least by separating Libya (to be ruled by Ptolemy VIII, who later invaded Egypt and became king between 145 and 116 BC – a supremely complex story of intrigue and murder in itself) from Egypt (to be ruled by Ptolemy VI and Kleopatra II).

It is not too much of an exaggeration to say that the Ptolemies rapidly descended into a pattern of murder, intrigue, and more murder – accompanied by frequent absconding with the contents of the royal treasury, and all the while Rome looked on.

By 96 BC, Rome had directly acquired the province of Cyrene (Libya) by the bequest of

OPPOSITE:
Portrait of Ptolemy I Soter, Greece or Asia Minor
A Macedonian general, Ptolemy (305–282) founded the Greek dynasty that bears his name some time after the death of his friend Alexander. Ptolemy added legitimacy to his governorship, and then rule, of Egypt by intercepting the body of Alexander and bringing it to Egypt. Alexander was probably buried at Alexandria, though his tomb still awaits discovery or identification. (Louvre Museum, Paris.)

a son of Ptolemy VIII, and so was positioned ominously on the western border of Egypt, but still the Ptolemies squabbled among themselves. When Ptolemy IX (88–80 BC; he had previously ruled between 116 and 107 BC) died, Rome wasted no time in sending a Ptolemaic protégé (a son of Ptolemy X), who had lived in Rome, to marry the widowed Berenike III (101–80 BC) as Ptolemy XI (80 BC). He quickly murdered the queen, only to be murdered in turn by the outraged Alexandrian mob. At this point, the Romans claimed that the recently deceased king had bequeathed Egypt to Rome – a claim that was unsurprisingly disputed in Alexandria, where a new Ptolemy (XII) and Kleopatra (V) were quickly installed amid increasing claims by Rome of 'illegitimacy'.

Ptolemy XII (80–58 BC) and Kleopatra V had several children: Berenike, a couple of Ptolemies, and two more daughters, Arsinoë and, in 69 BC, Kleopatra (destined to be Kleopatra VII or *the* Cleopatra).

Under Ptolemy XII, Egypt – trading as far as India and with the African interior – began to grow rich again, and by doing so attracted the even closer attention of Rome, whose armies were now not only on the western border of Egypt, but also close at hand in Judaea to the northeast. Explicitly presented with a large bill for being 'a friend and ally' of Rome in 60 BC, Ptolemy XII paid to keep his throne – a move that was so unpopular in Alexandria that he promptly lost it anyway, being replaced by Kleopatra V (58–57 BC) and her daughter Berenike IV (58–55 BC).

When Berenike IV became sole queen in 57 BC, Ptolemy XII – who in the meantime had visited Rome with his daughter Kleopatra – bribed the Roman general Pompey to send an army under Mark Antony to reinstall him on the Egyptian throne.

Part of this Roman force remained in Alexandria as Ptolemy XII's bodyguard, and some measure of stability was maintained during his second reign (55–51 BC). Indeed, the Great Library and Museum thrived, and the king ordered a new temple to be constructed at Dendera.

KLEOPATRA AND MARK ANTONY

In 52 BC, Ptolemy XII married his daughter Kleopatra VII (51–30 BC), who became ruler of Egypt the next year, when Ptolemy XII died, alongside Ptolemy XIII (51–47 BC). A gifted scholar and linguist, Kleopatra VII was determined to keep Egypt out of the hands of Rome – continuously and successfully seeking the support of the Egyptian priesthood in doing so – although the jealousy of her brother temporarily cost her the throne, as Rome acknowledged Ptolemy XIII as sole ruler in 48 BC.

Throughout this period, fighting between the Roman generals Pompey and Julius Caesar had allowed Egypt some breathing room, but when Pompey was finally defeated by Caesar he fled to Alexandria, to be followed by Caesar.

Learning that Pompey had been executed, Caesar took up residence in the royal palace and called for Ptolemy XIII and the displaced Kleopatra VII to appear before him. Caesar seems to have been thoroughly impressed by

OPPOSITE:
Portrait of Kleopatra VII, Rome
Now in the Altes Museum, Berlin, this portrait of Kleopatra VII (or Cleopatra; 51–30 BC) – effectively the last ruler of ancient Egypt – was found at a private villa near Rome. A gifted linguist and politician, Kleopatra manoeuvred in vain against Rome's desire to obtain Egypt. Her story – including the parts played by Julius Caesar, Mark Antony and Octavian (the future Emperor Augustus) – was to resonate around the world.

the 22-year-old queen, who was intelligent and self-confident, and he wasted no time in reinstating her as queen alongside an annoyed Ptolemy XIII. It was not a popular move, but Caesar protected Kleopatra in the ensuing bitter fighting in the Alexandrian streets, which ended when Ptolemy XIII drowned.

Instead of immediately annexing Egypt to Rome, Caesar allowed the now-pregnant Kleopatra to retain the Egyptian throne alongside her 12-year-old brother, Ptolemy XIV (47–44 BC).

Kleopatra and Caesar's son, known as Caesarion ('Little Caesar'), was born on 23 June 47 BC under the protection of three Roman legions left in Egypt by Caesar.

When he reached Rome in May 46 BC, Caesar – now a 'dictator' – sent for Kleopatra and installed her and their son for two years, as befitted their status, in a villa overlooking the city centre. Perhaps inevitably, the rumour developed in Rome that Caesar, together with Kleopatra, was intent on establishing a monarchy in Rome. This rumour was given credence when the Senate made Caesar 'dictator for life', and as a consequence he was assassinated by conspirators in March 44 BC, tipping Rome into chaos.

Kleopatra abruptly left Rome with her son and returned to Egypt, where she murdered Ptolemy XIV and made the three-year-old Caesarion (44–30 BC) co-ruler.

OPPOSITE:
First Pylon, Temple of Edfu
As Alexander had been, the Ptolemies were adept at absorbing those parts of ancient Egyptian culture that reinforced their grip on power. In particular, their astute adoption of the pharaoh's position within religious rites, and their favouring of the Egyptian priesthood, led to a major 'program' of temple building and restoration. The temple at Edfu was built between 237 and 57 BC, and is one of the best-preserved examples to have survived.

Meanwhile on the Roman stage, following the murder of Caesar, two factions emerged: one led by the assassins Brutus and Cassius, the other led by Caesar's confidant, Mark Antony and his heir, Octavian. Mark Antony had known Kleopatra in Egypt and called upon her now to assist him in the civil war, meeting with her at Tarsus.

Suitably impressed by the calculated opulence of Kleopatra's entourage, and, no doubt calculating for himself the uses to which he could put Egypt's wealth in the contest for the rule of Rome, Mark Antony followed Kleopatra to Alexandria. The tide was turning against him, however, and he was forced to return to Rome and agree to a truce – sealed by a marriage to Octavian's sister, Octavia.

THE DEATH OF KLEOPATRA

By 37 BC, Antony – as commander of the eastern Roman provinces – was in need of Kleopatra's help again (she had meanwhile given birth to their twins), and he and Kleopatra were married in Antioch in 32 BC (ill-advisedly, before Antony had divorced Octavia) – the Egyptian queen receiving large areas of the eastern Mediterranean as a wedding gift. Installed in Alexandria, Antony went further: donating further Roman territories to Kleopatra's children, and declaring Caesarion – and not Octavian – as the legitimate heir of Julius Caesar.

War was now inevitable.

In order to avoid the appearance of another Roman civil conflict, Octavian declared war on Kleopatra alone, although Antony was stripped of his power by the Senate. The clinching argument was evidence that Antony wished to be buried in Alexandria not in Rome.

The critical point of the war occurred on

2 September 31 BC at Actium in western Greece, where Antony and Kleopatra's forces, after a series of engagements on land and sea, were effectively beaten – although with heavy casualties on both sides. Kleopatra and Antony made a speedy return to Egypt. Octavian could not follow immediately, but did so by land and sea a year later. Antony was able to beat these forces back for a short period, but by 1 August 30 BC, Octavian was at the gates of Alexandria.

Antony committed suicide shortly afterwards – dying in Kleopatra's arms – and when Octavian entered the city, he placed Kleopatra under arrest. She committed suicide – most probably by poison rather than snakebite – on 10 or 12 August 30 BC. She was the last of the pharaohs, and Egypt was not to be a truly independent state again until AD 1952. Needless to say, Caesarion was murdered on 29 August 30 BC.

Egypt became a province of Rome and the personal property of Octavian (as the newly installed Emperor Augustus) and his successors.

THE END OF ANCIENT EGYPT

The period of Roman rule of Egypt that lasted until AD 395 was not overall a happy time for most Egyptians, who were thoroughly exploited by their new foreign and distant masters – although temples continued to be built or embellished, and many of the old rites continued for a time.

Those ancient rites and practices gradually lost their significance, however, as a new religion from another part of the Roman Empire, Christianity (traditionally believed to have been brought to Alexandria by the Apostle Mark around AD 50), gained ground – although not without its own difficulties.

The ancient temples were gradually abandoned to the desert or converted into churches (which ironically helped to preserve many of them through the centuries). The images of the ancient gods and goddesses were often scratched out by zealots – sometimes at considerable risk to their lives. The interpretation of the sacred language inscribed in hieroglyphs was lost completely.

For successive later rulers of Egypt, including the Arab elite who arrived in Egypt in 639–642, and the Ottoman Turks (from 1517), ancient Egypt was not part of their cultural heritage. Although their scholars were sometimes intrigued by the remains of the monuments around them, it is not unfair to say that often the only interest was in finding the gold of the ancients.

In Europe during the same centuries, ancient Egypt became a largely distant and distorted memory. It became a place associated mostly with manufactured magic rites and philosophy, but it was never entirely forgotten. By the eighteenth century, the occasional explorer had begun to describe the actual landscape and monuments of ancient Egypt, but it was only during the invasion of Egypt by Napoleon Bonaparte with his small army of accompanying *savants* (scientists and artists) in 1798–1801 that fact began to replace fiction about this most magnificent of ancient cultures.

OPPOSITE:
Statue of Horus, Temple of Edfu
Edfu was dedicated primarily to the falcon-headed god Horus, and to the goddess Hathor of Dendera – whose image would travel south from Dendera each year in a great festival marking their divine marriage. This 3m (10ft) black granite statue – one of a pair – guards the entrance to the hypostyle hall known as 'The Court of Offerings'.

LEFT:
Gayer-Anderson Cat, Memphis or Saqqara
This hollow, Late Period bronze cat, with a *wadjet* eye pectoral on its chest, earrings and a nose-ring is an iconic piece now to be found in the British Museum. The ancient Egyptians did not worship animals. The gods and goddesses were generally regarded as 'hidden' and 'unknowable'. A statue such as this simply represented a manifestation of the divine being – in this case, probably, the goddess Bastet.

OPPOSITE:
Mummy of a cat, Abydos
The mummification of animals – particularly cats (associated with Bastet) and ibises (associated with the god Thoth) – reached its peak during the Greco-Roman period in Egypt. The animals were bred in their thousands on temple estates to act as intermediaries between worshippers and the gods. The mummified remains were stored in vast catacombs such as those discovered at Saqqara, and elsewhere.

Entrance Gate, Temple of Dendera

The Temple of Hathor at Dendera was built in the Greco-Roman period, but there was a temple here from the Old Kingdom onwards. Due to a bend in the river, the temple faces north, rather than the more usual west–east alignment. The gateway shown here was built during the reigns of the Roman emperors Domitian (AD 81–96) and Trajan (AD 98–117).

Ceiling, Great Hypostyle Hall, Temple of Dendera
Dating to the reign of the Emperor Tiberius (AD 14–37), the beautiful outer hypostyle hall was constructed with 24 columns, each of which had a capital with the face of Hathor on each of the four sides. The ceiling maps out a symbolic chart of the heavens including the familiar signs of the zodiac, introduced to Egypt by the Romans.

OPPOSITE:

Dendera Zodiac, Temple of Dendera
On the roof of the temple, a small chapel dedicated to Osiris contained the celebrated Dendera Zodiac (it is now in the Louvre Museum, Paris). This unique circular map of the stars contains 12 signs of the zodiac – some in their familiar Greco-Roman form, and some in a more Egyptian style. On the outer ring, 36 figures symbolize the ancient Egyptian year of 360 days.

ABOVE:

Roman Birth House, Dendera
The Roman *mammisi* at Dendera follows the model of earlier Ptolemaic birth houses and was probably started by the Emperor Augustus (27–14 BC) soon after Egypt became part of the empire. The decoration, however, was added during the reign of Trajan. The birth house was associated with Ihy or Harsomptus, the son of Hathor and Horus.

PREVIOUS PAGES:

Hypostyle Hall, Temple of Esna
Esna was one of the last temples to be constructed during the Greco-Roman period, but only the hypostyle hall can be seen today. The back wall of the temple (the oldest part) dates to the reigns of Ptolemy VI (180–145 BC) and Ptolemy VIII (145–116 BC). The beautiful floral column capitals and walls of the Roman hypostyle hall continued to be decorated up to the third century AD.

RIGHT:

Kom Ombo Temple
Recent archaeological evidence suggests that Kom Ombo was the site of a temple from at least the Fourth Dynasty (2613–2494 BC), but the existing temple – the most elegant of the temples between Luxor and Aswan – dates from the reign of Ptolemy VI. Most of the decoration was added under Ptolemy XII (80–58 BC), and the Romans added a forecourt. The temple was dedicated primarily to the crocodile god Sobek – it is likely that the sand banks on the Nile nearby were a favourite resting place for crocodiles.

ABOVE:
First Pylon, Temple of Philae
No Egyptian temple has as fine a setting as the temple dedicated to Isis at Philae (the whole temple was moved to its present location in the 1960s to save it from disappearing below Lake Nasser). Although there is evidence of religious activities dating back to the reign of Taharqa (690–664 BC), the temple only became important in the Greco-Roman period, particularly as the worship of Isis spread throughout the Roman Empire.

OPPOSITE:
Rosetta Stone, Rashid (Rosetta), Nile Delta
The Rosetta Stone was found near Rashid by a French soldier attached to Napoleon's invasion force in July 1799, and proved to be key in the decipherment of hieroglyphs – knowledge of which disappeared from Egypt as Christianity spread throughout the country in the early centuries AD. The three inscriptions on the stone record a decree by Ptolemy V (205–180 BC) in hieroglyphs, demotic (a more easily written script based on hieroglyphs) and ancient Greek. Scholars soon recognized that the ancient Greek and hieroglyphic versions were likely to largely contain the same words. (British Museum, London.)

ABOVE:
Portrait of the Emperor Augustus, Arthribis
This marble portrait of Augustus (formerly known by the name Octavian) was found at Arthribis in Middle Egypt, and is now in the Greco-Roman Museum in Alexandria. After the death of Mark Antony and Kleopatra, Octavian formally annexed Egypt in the name of Rome. When he became emperor, however, Egypt became a personal province.

RIGHT:
'Trajan's Kiosk', Temple of Philae
This delightful structure lies to the east of the first pylon of the temple of Isis at Philae. Originally roofed in wood, the kiosk, of 14 columns connected by screen walls, was, for a time, the main entry point to the island. Although the decoration is usually ascribed to the Emperor Trajan, the structure may date to the reign of Augustus.

LEFT:

Catacombs of Kom el-Shuqafa, Alexandria

Much of the ancient city of Alexandria now lies below the shallow waters of the Mediterranean following seismic activity along the coast. Consequently, these fascinating catacombs give us a rare insight into late Ptolemaic and early Roman Alexandria. The art combines Greek styles with Egyptian religious rites, as can be seen here. The iconography is Egyptian, while the ceiling and the garlands are thoroughly Greek. The protective head of the gorgon Medusa also looks out from the central circle.

FOLLOWING PAGES:

Principal Tomb, Kom el-Shuqafa, Alexandria

Even at this late stage in ancient Egyptian history, the iconography within the catacombs of Kom el-Shuqafa is recognizable, though sometimes unusual. Here, on the right, an unidentified king or emperor presents the feather of the goddess Maat, representing justice, to the god Osiris – indicating, by extension, that the deceased has also been declared worthy of the afterlife. However, the hieroglyphs nearby no longer make sense, as knowledge of their meaning had already disappeared.

'Pompey's Pillar', Alexandria
This Roman triumphal pillar still stands in Alexandria – the largest such pillar, at 20.5m (67ft), constructed outside Rome and Constantinople. It stands above the ruined Serapeum – a temple constructed by Ptolemy III (246–222 BC) to the Greek-Egyptian god Serapis. The column was erected during the reign of the Emperor Diocletian (AD 286–305) to commemorate the Roman victory during a revolt by the city.

LEFT:
Funerary Portrait of Demos, Hawara, the Fayoum
Without doubt, the true jewels of Roman Egypt are the astonishing portraits that were originally attached to Roman Period mummy cases – especially those that were found at Hawara in the Fayoum. The mummy of this young woman, Demos (around AD 75–100), was found together with that of a little girl. An inscription states simply: 'Demos, aged 24, remembered forever.' (Egyptian Museum, Cairo.)

RIGHT:
Mummy of Artemidorus, Hawara, the Fayoum
This complete mummy case with the portrait in place (dating to around AD 98–117) was found undisturbed at Hawara with those of other family members, and is now in the British Museum. X-rays of the mummy suggest that Artemidorus was about 20 when he died. The Greek inscription says: 'Artemidoris, fare well!' Around the portrait there is a garland in gold leaf, and the scenes on the mummy case are gilded.

OPPOSITE:
Funerary Portrait of a Young Man, Hawara, the Fayoum
This fine portrait dating to the reign of the Emperor Hadrian (AD 117–138) is now in the Antikensammlung Museum, Munich, and beautifully encapsulates the melancholic aspect of these famous portraits. Nonetheless, it is easy to imagine what this man might have looked like in life.

ABOVE:
Temple of Kalabsha, near Aswan
Kalabsha – the largest free-standing temple in Upper Nubia – was dismantled in 1962–63 and moved to higher ground close to the Aswan High Dam. There may have been a temple here since the New Kingdom, but the visible temple was built in the last days of the Ptolemies and decorated during the reign of the Emperor Augustus. Like the temples at Kom Ombo and Edfu, Kalabsha was a healing temple where the sick would pray to the Nubian god Mandulis (among others) for relief.

Kom el-Dikka, Alexandria
The site of Kom el-Dikka allows archaeologists a rare opportunity to study a part of the city from the Ptolemaic Period through to the fourteenth century AD. In the early Greco-Roman period, the area was filled with large villas, though these were probably destroyed at the end of the third century during unrest in the city. By the sixth century, this area contained an academic complex of 22 Roman auditoria (left, distance) – the only ancient 'university' to have survived in the Mediterranean. The theatre in the foreground was originally an 'odeon' for musical performances.

ABOVE AND OPPOSITE:
Villa of the Birds, Kom el-Dikka, Alexandria
An early Roman villa at Kom el-Dikka contains a room – probably a cubiculum, or bedroom – in which the floor is composed of bird mosaics. Archaeological evidence, including the buckling of the blocks within the mosaics, suggests that the villa was destroyed by fire in the late third century. This may have been during unrest in the city in Diocletian's reign – the suppression of which was later celebrated by the building of 'Pompey's Pillar'.

RIGHT:
Offering Scene, Temple of Kalabsha
A number of Greco-Roman temples served as places where the sick and their families could pray to the gods for relief. Here, at the rear of the temple of Kalabsha, the Nubian god Mandulis (left), and an unidentified king, stand on either side of an offering table. The holes and grooves around the scene suggest that this was surrounded by a shrine before which the sick could pray.

FOLLOWING PAGES:
Sunset on the Nile
Without the Nile and its annual flood, ancient Egyptian civilization would not have existed. As it was appropriate to begin this book with an image of the sunrise over the Nile, so it is appropriate to end with an image of the last rays of the sun setting over the river. Together, we have briefly followed the ripples of time over 3000 years of history and art, but much more awaits the intrepid traveller in this most fascinating of countries today.

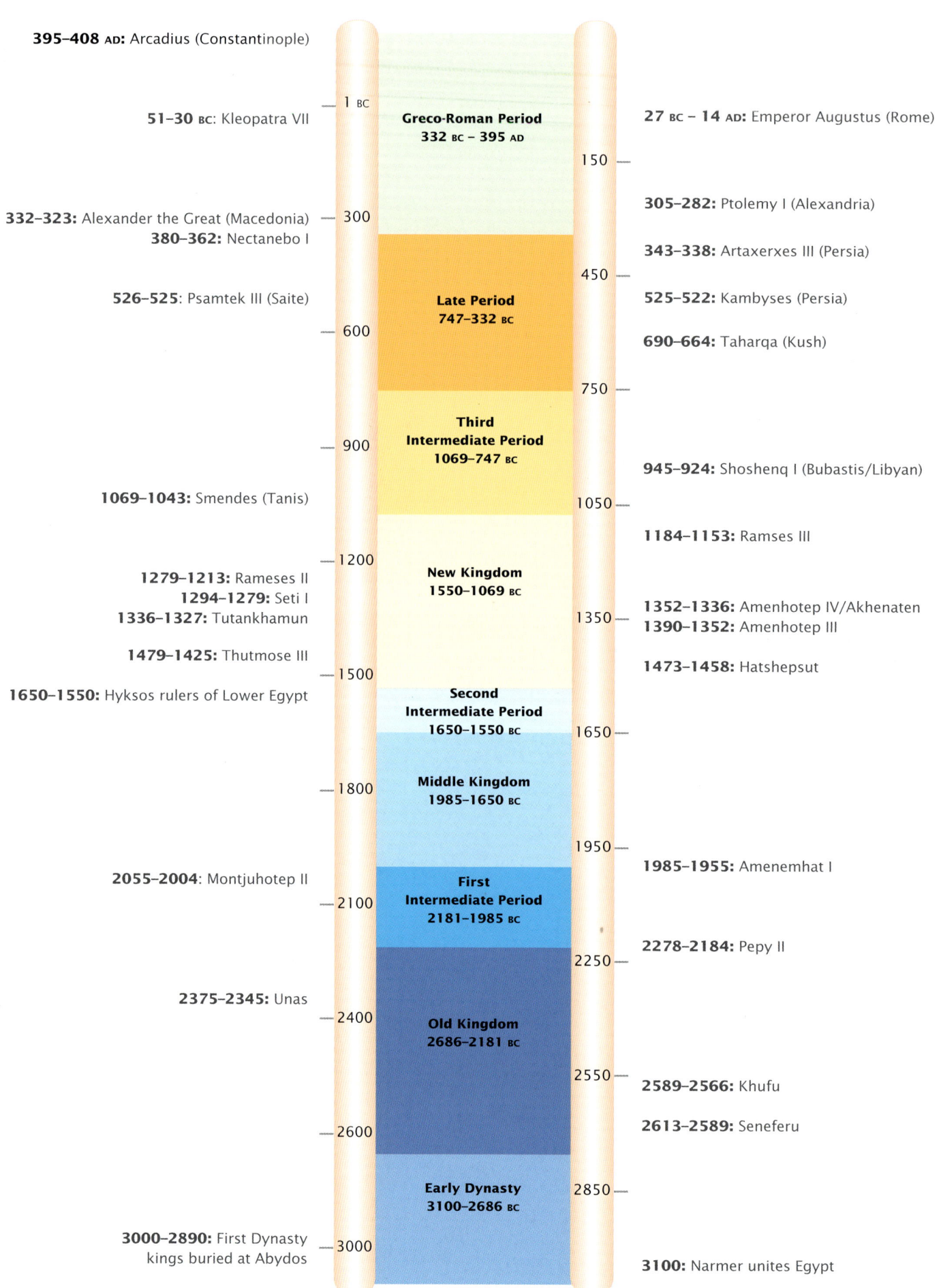

Acknowledgements/Picture Credits

AKG Images: 70 (Andrea Jemolo), 73 (Francois Guenet)

Alamy: 11 (Jose Lucas), 12 (Mike P Shepherd), 42 (Jose Lucas), 51 (Magica), 72 (David Tipling Photo Library), 77 (Prisma Archivo), 78 (HIP/C M Dixon), 85 (Prisma Archivo), 86 (Magica), 91 (Prisma Archivo), 96/97 (Artokoloro Quint Lox), 98 (Dallet-Alba), 99 (Peter Horree), 102 (World History Archive), 105 (Lebrecht), 108 (World History Archive), 109 (Prisma Archivo), 114 (Age Fotostock), 116 top (Robert Harding), 116 bottom (Lebrecht), 122/123 (Jim Henderson), 124 (Granger Collection), 125 (Interfoto), 126 bottom (Bildarchiv Monheim), 128/129 (Luis Dafos), 133 (Carolyn Clarke), 138 (Mike P Shepherd), 140/141 (Age Fotostock), 144 (De Rocker), 145 (Interfoto), 152 (BibleLand Pictures), 160 (Jim Henderson), 164 (Josse Christophel), 165 (Stefano Ravera), 166 (Age Fotostock), 173 (World History Archive), 181 (Lanmas), 182 (Azoor Photo), 188 (Peter Horree), 189 (Prisma Archivo), 195 (Nigel Westwood), 204/205 (Age Fotostock), 206/207 (Age Fotostock/Tono Labra), 210 (Interfoto), 211 (Granger Collection), 212 (VPC Photo), 218/219 (Panther Media)

Alamy/Heritage Images Partnership/Werner Forman: 63, 79, 103, 126 top, 157, 158, 162, 167–171 (all)

Bridgeman Images: 92 (Egyptian National Museum, Cairo)

Dreamstime: 18 (Mikhail Kokhanchikov), 21 (Shariff Chelah), 28/29 (Witr), 32/33 (Sue Martin), 34/35 (Lansbricae), 40/41 (Pius99), 46/47 (Don Mammoser), 58/59 (Maria1986nyc), 83 (Merydolla), 101 (Witr), 106/107 (Lapullka)

Christian Eckmann, Romisch-Germanisches Zentralmuseum, Mainz, Germany: 6

Nigel Fletcher-Jones: 15, 23, 24, 25, 36/37, 44/45, 49 (both), 50 (left), 57, 67, 74, 104, 111, 131, 146–149 (all), 200, 203, 217 (both), 220/221

Getty Images: 38/39 (Corbis Historical/Roger Wood), 43 (UIG/Universal History Archive), 60 (National Geographic/Kenneth Garrett), 65 (Heritage Images), 76 (The LIFE Images Collection/Barry Iverson), 115 (UIG), 120/121 (Robert Harding/Gavin Hellier), 127 (UIG/Werner Forman), 142 (S Vannini), 154 (UIG/Werner Forman), 155 (Burstein Collection), 172 (Corbis Historical/Roger Wood)

Getty Images/De Agostini: 50 (right) (Dagli Orti), 52 (G Sioen), 55 & 66 (Dagli Orti), 68 (M Seemuller), 69, 80 & 118/119 & 134 (S Vannini), 135 (Dagli Orti), 136 (G Oigolini), 139 (W Buss), 156 (A Jemolo), 194, 202 (S Vannini)

Metropolitan Museum of Art, New York: 22, 26/27, 61, 62, 64, 71 (both), 75, 143, 151

Shutterstock: 8 (Przemyslaw Skibinski), 10 (S-F), 30/31 (Sculpies), 89 (Simev), 95 (Matej Hudovernik), 110 (Vladimir Wrangel), 112/113 (Sam Vaughan), 130 (Michelle B), 132 (Noemosu), 137 (Michelle B), 150 (Nestor Noci), 153 (Juan Aunion), 174/175 (Irina Zholudeva), 176/177 (Raimonds Romans Raymoonds), 178 (Spiroview), 184 (Bumihills), 186 (Julius Fekete), 190/191 (Andrey Popov), 192/193 (Nick Brundle), 196/197 (Paul Vinten), 198/199 (Elizbieta Sekowska), 201 (Marco Sardi), 208/209 (Kerenby), 213 (Nestor Noci), 214/215 & 216 (eFesenko)

Walters Art Museum, Baltimore: 100